# The Bells of the Blue Pagoda

The Strange Enchantment
of a Chinese Doctor

By
Jean Carter Cochran

**TEACH Services, Inc.**
PUBLISHING
www.TEACHServices.com • (800) 367-1844

World rights reserved. This book or any portion thereof may not be copied or reproduced in any form or manner whatever, except as provided by law, without the written permission of the publisher, except by a reviewer who may quote brief passages in a review.

This book was written to provide truthful information in regard to the subject matter covered. The author assumes full responsibility for the accuracy of all facts and quotations as cited in this book. The opinions expressed in this book are the author's personal views and interpretation of the Bible, Spirit of Prophecy, and/or contemporary authors and do not necessarily reflect those of TEACH Services, Inc.

This book is sold with the understanding that the publisher is not engaged in giving spiritual, legal, medical, or other professional advice. If authoritative advice is needed, the reader should seek the counsel of a competent professional.

Copyright © 2013 TEACH Services, Inc.
ISBN-13: 978-1-4796-0196-7 (Paperback)
ISBN-13: 978-1-4796-0197-4 (ePub)
ISBN-13: 978-1-4796-0198-1 (Kindle/Mobi)

Library of Congress Control Number: 2013939458

Published by

www.TEACHServices.com • (800) 367-1844

# To My Sister

"I never crossed your threshold with a grief,
But that I went without it; never came
Heart-hungry but you fed me, eased the blame,
And gave the sorrow solace and relief.
I never left you but I took away
The love that drew me to your side again
Through the wide door that never could remain
Quite closed between us for a single day."

—*Author Unknown.*

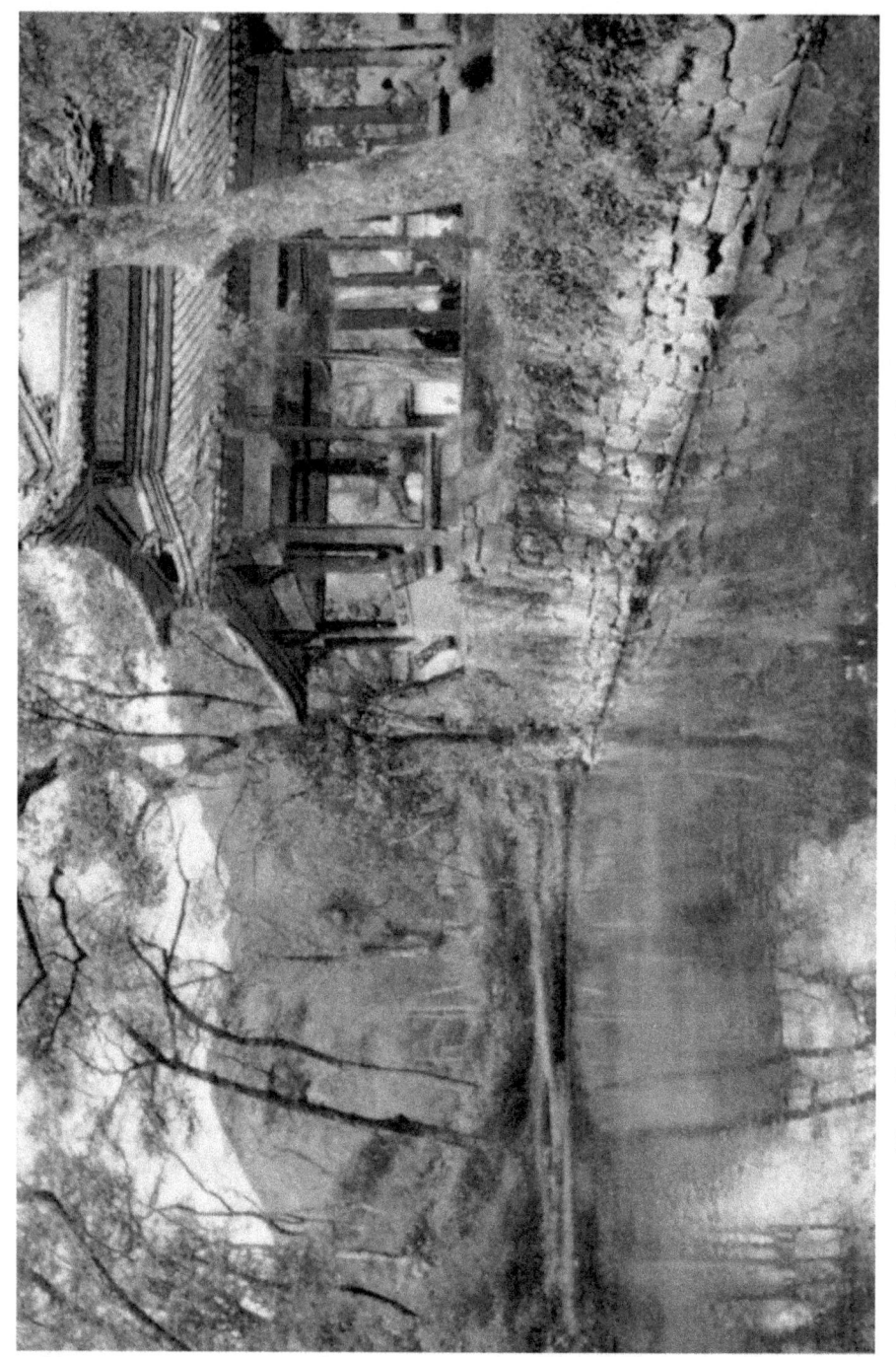

There In A Little Hollow, Shaded By Trees, Lay The Temple Of The Dragon Pool

# Introduction

It is no easy task to portray the life of a foreign land; with all the will in the world the writer is an outsider and often fails to realize the significance of some time-honored custom. All that the author can do is to try to catch the spirit of the country as best he may and the only recipe that one can give to him is that he should love the people and the country; otherwise he is doomed to failure. In this love there must be no lack of sincerity and one must endeavor to draw his characters as true to life as he would in writing of his own people.

This story is an attempt to catch the atmosphere and some of the poetry of China; for that reason the author has adhered to the Chinese custom of calling the characters and places by the picturesque names given as a matter of course in that country. Little Small-Feet, the Great Helpful Lady, and Old Scarred Face are examples of this. A book could be written on the artistic strain running through all Chinese literature that seems to prove China the most truly poetical country in the world.

Although the adventures of Little Small-Feet are imaginary, many of the incidents related were described to the author, who treasured up these events and wove them into one complete narrative. In China the occurrence that sounds the most improbable is the one of all others that is most apt to be true. In closing the writer would like to pay a tribute to Dr. Ida Kahn, Dr. Mary Stone, and many other Chinese women who are to-day the hope of their country in the self-denying, constructive work which they are doing. If anyone puts down this volume with a doubt as to the delightful, sterling qualities of the average Chinese man or woman, this book has failed to reflect the author's real feeling and purpose. She has endeavored in all that she has written to keep before her the ideals of one very near and dear who willingly laid down his own life that China might have light.

February 1, 1922.                                                                                                   J.C.C.

# Acknowledgements

In publishing this story the author wishes to acknowledge the kindness of Dr. Isaac Taylor Headland, who has allowed her to quote in full the poem, "Little Small-Feet," from his "Chinese Mother Goose Rhymes." Gratitude is also due to Dr. Headland for the material on Chinese training from his book, "Home Life in China," of which it may be said that there is no more amusing or instructive book on Chinese family life and education. His book on "Court Life in China" is a veritable classic on the subject and has been freely referred to in regard to funeral rites and ceremonies. Grateful acknowledgment is made of the courtesy of the publishers, Frederick A. Stokes Company, in granting permission to use, at the beginning of many of the chapters, lines from the poem by Alfred Noyes, "The Flower of Old Japan." The name, "Creeping Sin," was suggested by the character of that name in the same poem. Some of the photographs used are published in Shanghai by A. S. Watson and Company, and were taken by D. Mennie. Mr. Mennie's artistic photographs of China are a joy to all those who know the picturesque bits of the "The Flowery Kingdom," or, rather, "The Flowery Republic." Acknowledgment is also given to T. Hobbie for the use of a photograph.

# Table of Contents

|      | Introduction | v |
|------|---|---|
| I    | The Bells of the Blue Pagoda | 9 |
| II   | Creeping Sin | 18 |
| III  | In the Spider's Den | 26 |
| IV   | The City That Lies in the Shadow of Purple Mountain | 34 |
| V    | When Violets Came Again | 44 |
| VI   | Where the Hills Were Blue | 53 |
| VII  | Was It Creeping Sin? | 62 |
| VIII | Little Small-Feet Takes a Journey | 71 |
| IX   | The City of the Blue Pagoda | 81 |
| X    | The Deadly Pestilence | 91 |
| XI   | "The Terror By Night" | 102 |
| XII  | The Fearsome Caverns | 112 |
| XIII | Lord Chang Eats Bitterness | 122 |
| XIV  | "The Old Order Changeth" | 128 |
| XV   | A City Where Dreams Come True | 139 |

# Chapter I

# The Bells of the Blue Pagoda

> O, many a milk-white pigeon roams
>     The purple cherry crops,
> The mottled miles of pearly domes,
>     And blue pagoda tops,
> The river with its golden canes
>     And dark piratic dhows,
> To where beyond the twisting vanes
>     The burning mountain glows.
>
>     —Alfred Noyes.

The clusters of plum and cherry trees that covered the slopes of the little hills were a sea of bloom; Spring's dainty finger tips had run softly down each tender twig and tapering branch, and when she raised her hands, behold, in every place that she had touched there shone a blossom. Her little breezes, too, had played around the pomegranate thickets and turned them a deep red, and then had wandered away to tease the junks upon the river, at one moment blowing great gusts and the next leaving their sails hanging dejected and empty. These pranks were wanton mischief, for the truants knew very well that at this hour they were due at the old pagoda, to ring the fairy bells that hung from its carved balconies, and thus assure the anxious mothers who dwelt in the great walled city that the evil spirits were being frightened away and that their children would come to no harm.

Early in the morning, gentle Spring had warned the madcap breezes to be on the alert, and never to drift far away, for when green things were growing there was danger of spells and witchcraft and what was the use of building a pagoda on enchanted ground, if the bells were not kept constantly tinkling?

Certainly everything was auspicious so far as time and weather were concerned and yet there was trouble in the noble family of Chang. Could it possibly be that the little breezes were to blame? Old Wang Dah Mah, the amah, always maintained that if the pagoda bells had rung at the moment when Little Small-Feet was born, the baby would have been the much desired son, instead of a third unwelcome girl.

Lord Chang, the little girl's father, was the most bitterly disappointed of all the family. To have no heir to offer sacrifices before the family ancestral tablet was worse than unfortunate; it was a calamity. Nevertheless he allowed no sign of the storm of rage that shook him to appear on his immobile features; he could never forget the dignity that befitted him as a gentleman of rank. "What use have we for another girl? I shall be ruined by all these marriage portions; we had better put her away," he exclaimed in a hard voice, and at the same time broke the fan he was holding into bits between his long, slender fingers.

"Ah, no, only the very poor should employ those methods!" cried his wife. "Give my baby me." Poor Lady Chang! Added to her own sorrow was the realization that she was considered at fault.

Little Small-Feet herself, cuddled up warm to her mother's side, was absolutely oblivious to the coolness of her reception to the land of apricot blossoms, yellow dragons, and blue pagodas.

Only in the servant's quarters was the matter longer discussed. Long ago the ever wily Lord Chang had forbidden mention of the term "boy" in the house, for fear that the hovering, malignant spirits would come to realize on what his hopes were builded and out of sheer malice keep the longed-for heir away. But now among the underlings Wang Dah Mah aired her views very freely, and all her friends agreed with her that the silence of the pagoda bells boded no good to anyone.

"If only those bells had rung, things would be different in these courts today," Wang Dah Mah would shake her head and say. "No one would listen to me, however, but that is always the way—great people need no advice." Which was really scarcely fair, as Wang Dah Mah had never thought of suggesting such an expedient until Little Small-Feet had uttered her first cry.

Under old Wang Dah Mah's blue cotton coat beat a warm, motherly heart, and she looked after the little newcomer's welfare so carefully that the baby throve like the spring flowers on the mountain side. Out in the courtyard, where the flowering almond scented the air, by the miniature pond where goldfish played, the faithful amah would sit by the hour with her charge in her arms, croning nursery rimes in a cracked falsetto voice. One song, above all others, seemed to attract the baby's attention, for she would coo and laugh when it was sung:

> "The small-footed girl
>   With the sweet little smile,
> She loves to eat sugar
>   And sweets all the while.

> Her money's all gone
>   And because she can't buy,
> She holds her small feet
>   While she sits down to cry."

When it was ended the little one gurgled and smiled and, as she grew older, tried to hold up her tiny toes for inspection in such a knowing manner that then and there Wang Dah Mah began to call her Little Small-Feet. It made no difference that the baby's parents had chosen the name of Kwan Yin—Bright Mercy—as a pretty compliment to the Goddess of Mercy; that was soon forgotten and Little Small-Feet the baby became.

Spring's mischievous breezes had swept the last pink petal from the plum and peach trees and were rippling the soft, green sea of rice, when the first great event happened in Little Small-Feet's life. One April morning there was a stir and bustle in the women's court of the Chang palace. Caterers had been busy for days making toothsome dainties, salting almonds and watermelon seeds, and sugaring ginger and slices of oranges, not to mention the weightier matters of digging up long-buried eggs from their hidden stores and stewing shark fins and slimy sea slugs, in preparation for a formal feast that was to celebrate the day when Little Small-Feet was one month old. The excitement had spread beyond the walls of the palace of the Changs, over curved tile roofs and through circular doorways, into other palaces and homes, where official wives and ladies of high degree were all busy making ready to do honor to the occasion by their august presence. Seldom have been seen such reds and blues, and satins that would stand alone, stiff with the most gorgeous embroideries. There were long chains, and rings and pins of jade, and gay head ornaments, and tiny, beautifully embroidered shoes that were to adorn their "golden lilies." A feast at the Changs' was an occasion indeed and not to be entered into without much thought and many flutterings.

For the third time the runners had been sent out to summon them, and now at length the guests knew that the time of the feast was truly upon them and they must go. So each lady, supported by the hand of a maid, toddled on her tiny feet to her waiting chair and was duly assisted to enter by her attendants. The shades were nicely adjusted so that the luxurious passenger could see out, but with care that no curious eye could peep in upon her, and then the order to depart was given.

Sedan chair after sedan chair of the most gorgeous appearance was carried through the wide-open gates of the Chang palace. Little Small-Feet's mother, as gay as any butterfly, stood to greet her guests at the exact spot in the court that etiquette demanded and, bowing deeply, conducted them to the reception room. All was smiles, good cheer, and politeness, though somewhere in the background of each lady's mind ran the refrain: "It should have been a boy! It should have been a boy!"

"Such a fuss over the 'little happiness' of an unwelcome girl," whispered shrewish old Li Tai Tai to a neighbor when the hostess could not hear. "They never would have had this feast—I know old Chang too well—had it not been that the presents more than compensate for the cost of the feast. He has never wasted a cash; every one he spends brings in two at the very least."

Old Li Tai Tai had spoken truly, for Little Small-Feet was showered with gifts, all of them handsome and costly. There were solid silver and gold ornaments, embroidered coats, and many other things too numerous to mention.

When everything was ready for the ceremony Little Small-Feet was divested of her swaddling clothes and dressed in a bright-red dress, while an admiring group of ladies watched and commented.

"Ah!" exclaimed a guest, "I think she will be very beautiful. See how tiny her hands and feet are, and how her eyes sparkle."

"Yes," replied old Lady Li, who was wont to take a gloomy view of things, and who prided herself on her knowledge of proverbs and wise saws, "but the saying is, 'The beautiful bird gets caged.'"

"That's the reason, I suppose," tittered a pretty young wife in an aside to another, "that Li Tai Tai is so free to go back and forth at will; no one would think it worth while to cage her."

Unfortunately Li Tai Tai heard this remark and the black scowl she gave threatened a terrible storm, but at this moment Little Small-Feet began to scream herself, which diverted the old lady's attention. Thus far in the ceremony the baby had submitted with a good grace, but when these strange elders of hers started to shave her head, she felt that this was one thing no self respecting infant could stand, and she objected with the whole force of her young lungs. If Little Small-Feet had arrived at years of discretion she would have realized how futile such a protest was; the heads of baby girls had been shaved for several thousand years and could she, the daughter of the great Lord Chang, hope to escape?

Old Li Tai Tai tried to quiet her by tactfully singing,

> "We keep a dog to watch the house,
> A pig is useful, too;
> We keep a cat to catch a mouse,

> But what can we do
> With a girl like you?"

Little Small-Feet, as if she realized that she had been insulted, cried louder than ever at this noise and the dreadful grimaces the old lady made, and refused to be comforted until old Wang Dah Mah had given her a stick of barley candy which she peacefully sucked. The shaving was then completed, and the usual two tiny tufts of hair were left on the top of her head to guard against the evil eye.

At this feast, too, Little Small-Feet was formally given the name Kwan Yin. This to be sure was only a milk name, to be changed later on in life, but in reality it was used only by Lord Chang, when he was particularly disagreeable. This happened frequently for he never could be brought to smile with favor upon his youngest daughter.

The months rolled peacefully by for Little Small-Feet in spite of her father's frowns. Irises followed the earlier blossoms, and then came the peonies with their long satin petals; after them came the roses, making the courtyard a veritable bower, and, when the heat was most intense, the lotus flowers bloomed in the ponds of the gardens. The courtyards and gardens of the palace formed a world in itself beyond which the women of the family seldom strayed, but they were content with their gilded cage.

The City of the Blue Pagoda was situated south of the great river, among beautiful mountains and fertile valleys with lovely groves of bamboo trees. Even in winter roses and violets bloomed, birds came down from the north, and herons, wild geese, and pheasants added to the picturesqueness of the landscape. The city was the birthplace of Lord Chang, and whenever he fell into official disgrace at court, he would retire thither until his misdeeds were forgotten, or until he could buy his way into some more profitable employment. His family resided here almost constantly, as his positions were usually of short duration and traveling took many weeks of discomfort and expense. At the time when Little Small-Feet came, her father was under a cloud because of some very shady transactions as governor of a province; these things were not done "in a corner" and the long-suffering people finally arose in their wrath and demanded his removal. All this had certainly not helped Lord Chang's disposition, and to soften his disappointment over these misfortunes he resorted to his old friend, the opium pipe.

The family enjoyed their home much better when official business called the gentleman of the household away. But for the first years of Little Small-Feet's existence he was constantly at home. The baby could not understand why he was the only one of the household from whom she could never win a smile, but it did not trouble her very much so long as all the rest of the world responded so eagerly.

Before the lotus blossoms began to fade on their long stems and the rice was garnered in from the hillside, Little Small-Feet had learned some very interesting things; one was that if she screamed long enough, doubled up her fists hard enough, and grew red enough in the face, she could have almost any mortal thing she wanted. Having learned these facts she very seldom failed to put the knowledge into use, and if it had not been for the natural sweetness of her disposition, she would have been terribly spoiled in a few years. Old Wang Dah Mah aided and abetted these practices for she was never known to refuse the child any desire.

"Little Small-Feet wanted it," was surely excuse enough.

At other times the baby would be smiling and winsome, her black eyes snapping, and she always had a gleeful laugh for anyone who played with her. When Wang Dah Mah dressed her in a bright-blue silk coat with little green trousers and hat and shoes embroidered in butterflies, she was such an entirely adorable infant that the little breezes could scarcely be persuaded to play any where but in the Changs' courtyard. They would blow softly over the poppies and the lotus ponds, making the flowers dance and bow just for the sake of hearing Little Small-Feet shout and clap her hands with glee, and of course they forgot entirely that the pagoda bells were hanging silent and that every mother's heart in the city was beating anxiously.

One day, however, when Little Small-Feet was two years old, gentle Spring made a great discovery. In the corner of the Changs' garden, on a hill which overlooked the city wall, the river, and the pagoda, was a beautiful tiled pavilion Among all the haunts in the garden, the baby liked this spot the best, because from it she could watch the stately junks with their fanlike sails, the pranks of the little breezes, and last but not least the blue pagoda, which she liked far better than anything she had ever played with; there were numberless stormy scenes because Wang Dah Mah would not give it to her as a toy.

Now gentle Spring discovered that Little Small-Feet fairly screamed with delight when ever she heard the music of the pagoda bells, so of course the friendly dame imparted the good news to her breezes and from that day forward the pagoda bells were ringing constantly.

Sad to confess, Little Small-Feet was very slow in learning to walk; it was so much easier to be carried around in the arms of the faithful Wang Dah Mah that probably she would never have attempted to use her own small feet had it not been for the delightful games which she saw her two older sisters playing. After watching them and their companions sitting in a circle, with their hands together in a fascinating game called "water the flowers," or happy over "flower seller," she wanted to join them, and at length she began to stand alone. And very soon her toddling steps led her into much mischief.

Slowly Little Small-Feet grew out of babyhood to girlhood, and all the time she was absorbing and learning, but not from books, for Wang Dah Mah was her chief teacher and she did not know the character for "man" from the character for "happiness." The amah taught her charge other things, however, such as respect to parents, how to bow to ladies who came to visit her mother, and countless polite sayings which it is necessary for girls of high rank to know. She was taught that the harm in lying lies in being found out, and to be careful never "to lose one's face." All these things the pupil picked up only too quickly. One point was often discussed between them, and that was about the pagoda; Little Small-Feet wished to go there but for once Wang Dah Mah absolutely refused to take her; instead she tried to frighten her out of her desire by horrid tales of evil spirits and demons. Wang Dah Mah absolutely believed these tales herself, and nothing would have induced her to visit the haunted ground on which the pagoda stood.

One beautiful autumn day when Little Small-Feet was four and a half years old, she sat in the pavilion, listening to the pagoda bells, and watching a flock of wild geese arriving from the north for the winter. An overmastering longing to see that beautiful blue tower nearer at hand came over her; she must know how the bells sounded outside the city wall. Her heart began to heat wildly. Should she run away to the pagoda just for a short time? No one would miss her. Clutching a little toy she was playing with tightly in her hand, she slipped down to the other end of the garden, through the reception room where her father received his guests, through another court and still another. For once the usual well thronged house was empty; stranger yet, when she arrived at the great entrance gates, they stood a little ajar. On reaching the street she saw the reason for all this lack of runners and attendants; half a block away a group of strolling players were performing, and all the available population were gathered around intent on watching the actors.

Now that the moment of freedom had come, Little Small-Feet was rather embarrassed to know what to do; but as all her acquaintances were on one end of the street, instinct told her to turn the other way. Never before had she been on this path alone, or on foot, and the sensation was truly novel. The shops, the street signs, and the vendors were most fascinating, and she often stopped to look and listen. The thought of the pagoda, however, drew her ever forward, an by sheer chance she took the few turns that led her to the great city gates set in the massive walls. This place was truly alarming, for beasts of burden, carts, and wheelbarrows were passing in and out in an unbroken stream. Little Small-Feet shrank back, thoroughly frightened, and was just in the act of turning and trotting home, when through the arch, a half mile or so away, she caught sight of the pagoda. Her courage and resolution returned, and keeping close to the wall, she slipped through the traffic and started out toward the alluring landmark.

By the time the last step to the pagoda was taken, Little Small-Feet was weary enough, and climbing up two flights of the steep stairs to the corner of the carved balcony, she curled up in a heap to listen to the bells and enjoy the sight of a fleet of beautiful ships in the river. The breezes must have realized that they had a guest that day, for they swung the bells back and forth with a will and to the sound of their silver tones she fell fast asleep.

Suddenly, much later, the wanderer awoke with a shiver to find that night was coming on with swift, noiseless tread, and out of the dark, in the chamber of the pagoda, she saw two bright, cruel eyes watching her. The child started forward with a shiver of terror. She must go home, and to do so she had to pass those never-winking eyes. All the stories of demons and evil spirits which Wang Dah Mah had told flashed into her mind. What should she do? If she was to get into the city before the gates were shut, she must start at once. With a mighty effort of will, the child ran into the room, past the gleaming eyes and down the two flights of stairs, hearing soft footsteps following her, accompanied by low snarls and growls. This gave wings to her feet and, never heeding what direction she took, she ran as fast as possible toward the city wall. Unfortunately poor Little Small-Feet in her terror took a road leading to another gate farther down toward the city, and this mistake changed all the course of her future existence. Where were the little breezes now, and what kind of friends were they, to desert her in her hour of need? And all the time during the little girl's flight the horrid dog followed, yapping and snarling. The breezes might have learned a lesson from his constancy.

As Little Small-Feet approached the city she came up to a group of itinerating beggars who were going in the same direction. On catching sight of this beautifully dressed child they turned at once and surrounded her. With rough voices and coarse oaths they spoke to her; too frightened to reply, she tried to hurry on. It was useless; dirty hands clutched and pulled her, and she was immediately threatened by a quarreling mob, more like a pack of dogs than human beings. One shrewish crone was the leader, and as the band seemed about to pull the poor child to pieces, the hag interfered:

"What stupidity is this; shall we obtain money for these gay clothes if we tear them all to rags? They are worth several taels at the very least. We will take her and hide her for a ransom, which will come to more than a thousand suits such as this."

"Yes, Old Scarred Face, and never a cash of it shall we see, for you and Creeping Sin will pocket it all; 'spilt water cannot be gathered up again'; let each take something now; I for one will have the coat."

At the name of Creeping Sin, Old Scarred Face turned livid with fear and rage. Had the connection between them been discovered? If so, a great chance for their profit was gone. "You cow," she raged, "if you all get fighting over the garments there won't be a thread to take to the pawnbroker's to sell; you know that without my help you would be in prison to-day, instead of the most prosperous band of beggars on this side of the Yang-tse-Kiang. I shall leave you all to make what you can without me," and she started to go.

Knowing that she spoke the truth, they would not let her go, but said that they would follow her advice. Thereupon she put the poor, terror-stricken Little Small-Feet in their midst, where she would be unobserved by passers-by, and hurried the party along to a group of dirty mat-shed hovels huddled at the base of the city walls. In this particular vicinity there were thousands of these huts, and he would be a brave man indeed who would dare to enter this district and search for anyone.

In all that vast city no heart was so desolate as Little Small-Feet's; instead of the rich fare of the palace, the dirty rice from a beggar's bowl was to be her portion. She could not even cry for Old Scarred Face told her that she would tear her limb from limb if she shed but one tear, and Little Small-Feet realized that silence was a necessity. No rich bed was her pallet but a bundle of loathsome straw, and worst of all there was no doting Wang Dah Mah to comfort her and quiet her fears. Surely her old amah had been right when she had told her charge that the blue pagoda was an ill place to seek.

Little breezes, little breezes, you may well ring the pagoda bells softly and sadly as if for a passing soul, for henceforward you will seek in vain for a playmate in the winding paths of the garden or by the pool of goldfish. No childish hands will be clapped in glee at the dancing poppies and waving fields of rice for Little Small-Feet has turned into a somber highway, the road of tears and sorrow, the road down which many tiny, childish feet have trod and very few returned, the road to beggar land.

# Chapter II

# Creeping Sin

> Because the white-faced mandarin
>   Would dog our steps for many a mile,
>   And sit upon each purple stile
>   Before we came to it, and smile
> And smile; his name was Creeping Sin.
>
> His grin was very sleek and sly:
> Timidly we passed him by.
>   He did not seem at all to care:
> So, thinking we were safely past,
> We ventured to look back at last.
>   O, dreadful blank!—He was not there!
>
> —Alfred Noyes.

That night the sun dropped suddenly to rest in a heavy bank of gray clouds, and soon a violent wind arose, far different from the soft breath of the little breezes, and shrieked like a wolf through the streets of the city, tearing down signs and scattering loose tiles in every direction. Like frightened birds, the junks upon the river scurried into shelter, and the high waves beating against the shore threatened to sink them as they lay at anchor.

Late in the evening the rain began to fall in torrents, so that the frail walls of the hut where Little Small-Feet lay were nearly washed away. The water ran in a stream under the straw on which she slept, and the wind's wild wail was a startling contrast to Wang Dah Mah's crooning cradle song. It was no wonder that the lost one awakened from her troubled sleep screaming with fear. Fortunately for her, her jailers slept soundly, for had she aroused them, a speedy retribution would have followed.

Old Scarred Face had left the hut some hours before, putting the child under the custody of the other mendicants, while with crafty intent she turned her footsteps cityward. The great city gates were about to swing to for the night, when she pushed her way boldly through, along with a score of other belated travelers. She resembled nothing so much as an animated scarecrow: as she strode along with her staff in one hand, her beggar's bowl in the other, and her little mongrel cur following at her heels, but she attracted no particular attention as there were many other such figures roaming the streets. Already the wind had begun to moan and passers-by were hurrying home to shelter before the rain should fall, but unconscious of wind and weather the woman plied her trade, holding out her bowl with a detestable whine, which arose into a curse when she asked in vain. All the time her senses were on the alert to pick up fragments of gossip that might give her some clue to the identity of Little Small-Feet.

Wayfarers were in far too much of a hurry, however, on this stormy evening, to stay and retail news. There was no cluster of idlers in front of the tea shops or at the corners, and she dared not stop pedestrians and ask them questions for fear of arousing suspicions, so she was forced to content herself by reviling them in her heart with many fearful oaths.

After an hour or two of aimless wanderings, Old Scarred Face came to the part of the town where the gentry resided and found, outside of one of the largest gateways, an excited knot of people. In an indifferent manner she approached the outskirts of the crowd and listened to the discussion. It did not take her long to determine that here was the place to find the information she sought.

"It's Little Small-Feet, I say, Little Small-Feet and she has been stolen, or else the evil spirits have carried her away," wailed a respectable-looking woman, the center of the group. "They did not have the pagoda bells rung at her birth and this is the result. I always told them how it would end. She was no ordinary child, and now I know that she was a changeling!" and she began to cry in good earnest.

These words of Wang Dah Mah made the crowd feel that this was a serious matter indeed and not to be lightly discussed. At the words "evil spirits" each one looked over his shoulder apprehensively to see that no such ill-omened specters were lurking behind him. To Old Scarred Face the news was honey and nectar; this was at last the intelligence she sought.

"Whose child is lost?" she inquired of one of the servants standing at her elbow.

"It is strange that you should not have heard," he replied; "Lord Chang's little girl has been stolen away, or perhaps, as Wang Dah Mah believes, the spirits have carried her to their own country."

At the name of Lord Chang, a gleam appeared in the eyes of Old Scarred Face. Here was booty indeed!

"And what is the reward?" she inquired, a shade too eagerly.

The man turned on her with suspicion: "No reward at all, if I know anything about the man. But why do you want to know? I believe you stole her yourself, you hag."

Old Scarred Face was in greater danger now than she had ever been before. But just as the man started a hue and cry against her, the rain began to fall in such torrents that all were forced to run for shelter, and in the midst of the confusion the beggar woman disappeared.

The cunning builders of the City of the Blue Pagoda took no chances with fate, but had carefully laid out the streets to foil the dread designs of malicious spirits. The spirits as a whole must be rather dull, for though they can travel with ease and swiftness down a straight highway, they are at once bewildered when it comes to a curve. All the thoroughfares, therefore, were planned to curve and wind in a fashion that was confusing to many besides the crafty demons.

It was wonderful how Old Scarred Face kept her course in the teeth of the gale. With as little hesitation as a mole runs through the passages and underground galleries of the earth, she picked her way down the Lane of Filial Piety, across Duck Street, and up the Alley of Happiness, on and on through a veritable labyrinth of lanes and alleys, until in the very heart of the maze she halted before a blank wall that stood in front of a gateway. Here again the plots of evil spirits were to be frustrated, for with all their knowledge of the world and of infernal regions, the wicked ones are unable to go around such a wall and enter the house. In this instance, however, the plan seemed to have failed, or perchance the mischief-makers had some other mode of entrance, for throughout the length and breadth of the Flowery Kingdom, it would be hard to find a place so full of every form of plot and evil design as this building before which Old Scarred Face had stopped.

The beggar woman did not falter a moment but, going boldly up to the gate, gave three short raps and in a moment rapped again. It was apparently a signal, for the gateman appeared immediately, and with no sign of surprise allowed the woman to come in. As she stood under the protecting eaves of the gatehouse the vagrant gave herself a shake like a huge Newfoundland puppy and drew a dirty hand across her eyes in order to clear her vision from raindrops. No greater contrast could be imagined than the ragged, drenched mendicant with her yellow dog slinking at her heels and the spacious, luxurious court she now entered. Now and again, when the rain lifted its veil, distant vistas of winding paths and rockeries could be seen, with here and there a goldfish pool, or flower beds of gay chrysanthemums, while at the other end of the court the ornate lines of a stately guest room were visible.

Old Scarred Face had no desire to be shown thither, however, and with a nod to the attendant she slipped through a round archway that stood on one side of the garden, down a narrow stair way, and by an underground hallway through a maze of rooms and larger apartments. At length she came to a curiously wrought iron door that seemed absolutely soundproof, and above it hung a rope which she pulled very slowly. As she stood waiting, a bat disturbed by the noise brushed her with its wings as it flew past.

"Ha! A bat! A good omen!" she exclaimed; "I knew my luck had turned." After a moment the door opened a few inches, and an inquiring face appeared in the aperture; then the door was thrown back by a humpbacked dwarf who leered up into the hag's face in a most revolting fashion.

Poor Little Small-Feet, to what a pass had she now come, that her fortunes should be discussed in such a den as this!

Few of the inhabitants of the City of the Blue Pagoda would have had the hardihood to enter that doorway, but Old Scarred Face was unafraid. Two guttered candles and a charcoal brazier threw a flickering light into the center of the room, leaving the corners in darkness; in one of these the dwarf gibbered to himself, while above one could hear the scurrying feet of rats made restless by the storm. The walls and ceilings were draped in cobwebs in lieu of costly tapestry, and a sickish odor of a powerful drug made the smoky air still heavier.

A man was seated at a rickety table, on which the two candlesticks stood. At first glance he seemed a strange inmate for such an apartment; he was clad in costly silks, his queue was neatly plaited, and his shapely hands an long, carefully guarded nails all proclaimed him a gentleman. A single look, however, at his masklike face and crafty eyes was enough to awaken in the observer suspicion and dislike. He did not move when Old Scarred Face entered; but allowed her to remain unnoticed for several minutes.

"Well, what do you want here?" he finally drawled while he looked her up and down with an insufferable smile.

Ah! be careful, Creeping Sin, for Old Scarred Face holds trump cards tonight, and she knows it!

"It is nothing," she answered and turned to go.

The Road to Beggar Land

The man perceived his mistake and called her back with the inquiry, "Have you eaten rice to-night?"

"Eaten rice! Where could a woman find rice a night like this? Can it grow in streets ankle deep in water?"

Creeping Sin thereupon ordered the dwarf, who had just enough intelligence to understand his commands, to go and fill her bowl in the kitchen.

"What is the news of the road and the great game?" asked the man with the same sly smile. "Did the last consignment of flowers reach the City on the Sea in safety?"

"All but two of the imbeciles, and they the most handsome! The silly girls preferred the river for a bed, and threw themselves in when I was not looking. One cannot be everywhere at once," growled the woman. "I only made a paltry shoe or two on the whole transaction, and look at the risk I ran. I shall not dare show myself at the North Capital for many a long day."

"Never do what you would not have known," replied her host unctuously.

The woman's temper had gradually been rising. "That is too much from you! You whom we all call Creeping Sin! You who sit like a great, fat spider in his den, weaving a web to catch flies and moths to the uttermost part of the Middle Kingdom! They say you even have messengers in foreign lands, and send these slaves to the City by the Golden Gate. Is it true? Is it true?" and her voice rose to a perfect scream.

Alarmed by her violence Creeping Sin changed his tactics. "Some day I will tell you, and you will perhaps unite in a game of even greater profit, but just now I have some news of some country girls whom we might easily kidnap."

"Why do you say 'we' when you mean me? I take all the danger and hardships of the business, while you live in luxury and ease and will not so much as allow me to enter your palace. Instead you bring me to this cavern, and I am not good enough to go in at your front gate. I did to-night, however, and will whenever I choose!"

Creeping Sin turned a shade darker, and a malignant look replaced the crafty smile. "You may use the road at your pleasure, but it will not be for long, for I know of a certainty that the gate is marked, and your comings and goings will be watched with interest by eyes that will have to be heavily bought to keep them closed. Lord Chang has nothing to do and he is on the alert for even very small, skinny fish. As for my living in luxury, it is widely reported that your wealth far exceeds my little savings, and whenever you wish to dig it out of those caves in which you have it hidden, you are your own mistress, and can do it. If, as you choose to imply, my reputation is not above reproach, how about your own? Remember, I could reveal a great deal, and if you continue as you have begun, it will take many shoes to keep me quiet."

This threat sobered Old Scarred Face and the beggar's whine returned to her tone. "Everyone knows that 'tigers and deer do not stroll together,' so it is safest for us both to hold our peace. The front gate was unwatched to-night; no one was on the street. I did not even hear the watchman's drum that warns thieves not to steal and rob because he is on the alert. But I have come with good tidings and we are wasting precious time. Guess whom I now have in my toils; nay, I will tell you for it is too good to keep. Lord Chang himself, and no other! At last he shall rue having cast me into prison, and the sum I paid to go free he shall repay a thousandfold!" At the thought of her enemy Old Scarred Face reviled most horribly.

Creeping Sin waited until her paroxysm had passed, and sat very much like a wise spider gloating over its victim. In his innermost heart he knew that the only way to rid himself of this accomplice and all that she knew of his plans, was to kill her, and at present she was too useful for him to contemplate such a course. Therefore he humored her, and egged her on, but all the time he mentally added up the score he had against her, to be paid with interest when the day of reckoning came.

After a moment or two, Old Scarred Face recovered enough to tell the story of Little Small-Feet. As Creeping Sin listened, he allowed no sign of pleasure to disturb his masklike countenance, although inwardly he exulted over the happy chance that had thrown his archenemy, Lord Chang, into his power.

"You say you will not take less than twenty thousand taels by way of reward?" said Creeping Sin. "How do you expect to get it? You can not treat with the man himself; you would rest twenty years in jail if you attempted it. I see your scheme; you want me to play the middleman and go-between; but it will take many middlemen to lay this before the father, and the cost will be heavy. I will attempt it only upon condition of reaping two thirds of the ransom."

"Two thirds of the ransom! Hear him, hear him!" woman shrieked. "The brigand, the pirate, robber of poor starving widows, and of the virtuous! Goddess of Mercy, hear and avenge the helpless!"

The battle raged almost the whole night through, but at length toward morning the worthy pair came to an understanding, one that they had known in the beginning would be the final arrangement. The profits were to be divided between them and until the negotiations could he successfully completed, Little Small-Feet was to be placed under the care of Creeping Sin. Old Scarred Face was very suspicious of this arrangement but was forced to comply because the man refused to consider any other plan.

"You know full well that you will starve her if you keep her," he insisted. "You never yet have fed anyone enough to keep body and soul together, not even yourself, and if we return the child badly treated, we are likely to run into danger."

When Old Scarred Face had consented to this arrangement, and had promised to bring Little Small-Feet the following evening to the Spider's den, Creeping Sin withdrew to his luxurious quarters above ground, leaving the woman to make herself as comfortable as possible where she was, for she could not go from the city until the gates were opened in the morning.

Thus was Little Small-Feet's fate decided by these crafty and cruel conspirators, who never showed their victims any pity, and who never expected to receive compassion should they them selves be caught in the toils. Was it an omen of the future that the soft, friendly breezes of the summer had fled before the shrill, shrieking blast of typhoon and of storm? Or could Kwan Yin have taken this full revenge on the helpless one who, through no fault of her own, had discarded the goddess' name?

# Chapter III

# In the Spider's Den

> He played with children's beating hearts,
> And stuck them full of poisoned darts
>    And long green thorns that stabbed and stung;
> He'd watch until we tried to speak,
> Then thrust inside his pasty cheek
>    His long, white, slimy tongue:
> And smile at everything we said;
> And sometimes pat us on the head,
>    And say that we were very young.
>
>           —Alfred Noyes.

The City of the Blue Pagoda no longer lay smiling under the caresses of gentle Spring or shimmering in the heat of an August sun. The dreams that lay in the hearts of the poppies had all been gathered by eager, clutching fingers, and the last crop of rice lay on the threshing floor. The pagoda itself, which stood as sentinel over the fears of the mothers of little children, had surely forgotten the purpose for which it was erected, for from the mountains back of the river wild animals descended upon the town with shrieks that sounded like souls in torment. All the demons that lurked in cavern and grotto seemed to be at large, wailing over roofs and twisting their way mercilessly down crooked streets that had been so craftily planned to prevent their entrance. At moments there would come a lull in the tempest and the inhabitants would draw a sigh of relief, thinking that their tormentors had retreated to their mountain caves, when a blast still more alarming would shake the pagoda to its very foundations and threaten to lay the city in ruins.

Throughout the raging of the tempest, Lady Chang and Wang Dah Mah were beside themselves with fear for the fate of their darling. Wang Dah Mah had to be restrained almost by force from roaming the streets in search of Little Small-Feet, while Lady Chang, regardless of wind and rain, ran up and down the garden paths and peered anxiously into the goldfish ponds and into every summer house, in the vain hope that her child might be found hidden in some corner. The search continued long after the storm had abated and the sun had returned to shine on the ravages of the typhoon, At first Lord Chang appeared as eager as the most zealous and sent out criers in every direction. One day, however, he told his wife that on the night preceding the typhoon a child exactly answering Little Small-Feet's description had been seen to fall into the river, and had been swept away by the current. And from that hour he ordered all attempts to find the little one to be abandoned.

This was sad news to an undisciplined mother's heart, and Lady Chang and Wang Dah Mah gave vent to their grief in piercing wails and shrieks.. The nights of unrestrained weeping nearly exhausted Lady Chang and the family became alarmed and Lord Chang very angry. Such fretting for an unwelcome girl was unseemly and would make them a laughingstock throughout the city. The mourning must cease. Outward demonstration being denied her, the poor mother pined in secret, and there seemed danger of her following her little daughter into the great unknown. At last Wang Dah Mah came to the rescue.

"It is many months since we have made a pilgrimage to the Temple of the Dragon Pool," she suggested. "Perhaps the Goddess of Mercy is angry at us for so long neglecting her, and besides the priest in the temple may be able to comfort us and tell us if we shall ever see our darling again."

The thought of such an undertaking aroused the interest of the drooping lady. Sedan chairs were brought out and the bearers ordered to be in readiness. The chairs holding Wang Dah Mah, Lady Chang, and her two daughters, with those of the ladies in waiting, made quite a procession as they left the city gates and wound their way up the mountain side. The bamboo groves were still green and cast their feathery shadows over the path as they passed along. The birds in all the thickets and tangled grasses sang as lustily as though no storms could ever befall them, and gay lizards darted across the road. As they went higher and higher wonderful views of river and city spread like a map before their eyes; the high wall, the red roof of the drum tower and gates, with the tiles of the houses and the tapering blue pagoda, made a scene full of color that delighted the spectators. The sun was very warm, and its kindly radiance also comforted the lady's heart. After a three hours' climb the bearers suddenly made a turn around the shoulder of the mountain, and there in a little hollow shaded by willow and bamboo trees lay the Temple of the Dragon Pool.

The long rays of the afternoon sun touched one side of the pool, and in the other were reflected the quivering leaves of the graceful trees and the curves of the temple roof. Here, surely, one could find peace!

Aware that some great personage approached, the attendants ran out of the temple and with many bows besought the ladies to alight. Lady Chang sent the children with her ladies in waiting to sit beside the lake, while she and Wang Dah Mah proceeded to mount the steps of the shrine and talk to the priest. When she had entered the building, she turned to the priest and told him the story of Little Small-Feet's disappearance and death.

"Tell me, I beseech you," she implored, "that in some other life I shall hold my precious one in my arms again."

"That is a foolish and wicked wish," replied the priest. "You must not speak of her here or the gods will be angry and visit their wrath upon us. It will take many cash and much incense to purify the air after such words. Do you not understand that your little girl was not a child at all but a changeling or demon? If she had been human, she would never have disappeared in that way. The spirits, you say yourself, howled long with glee that she had joined them at last. It is a grievous sin even to think of her, and the only hope for you is to pray for a son and heir." Poor Lady Chang, she had come for bread and had been given a stone! How could she know that a messenger of Lord Chang had come by a nearer and shorter way to instruct the priest how to answer her?

With a deep sigh the Lady mounted to the Goddess of Mercy's shrine and burned incense and paid for the necessary prayers to be said. She and Wang Dah Mah each took a vow never again to taste the flesh of any bird that had flown through the air, hoping that this self-sacrifice might perhaps guard the other children from evil, and so propitiate the goddess that she would give to the mother the great desire of her life, a little son. Then, weary and sad, she gave the word of command to return home.

The day was waning fast, and the warm sun was setting, giving place to a cold wind from the mountain that struck chill to the bones, and moaned through the branches of the trees. The bearers quickened their pace and Lady Chang pulled down her blinds and, huddling back in her chair, gave way to her grief and desolation.

After this journey, all hopes of seeing Little Small-Feet again were laid aside, and the old life that they had known before the child came was resumed. No stranger would have suspected any difference. The women dressed and ate, gossiped and embroidered, as formerly, but a close observer might have noticed that when the pagoda bells were silent, Lady Chang and Wang Dah Mah were restless and excited and could not bear the older children out of their sight for a minute, and could any have seen into their hearts, they would have beheld scars that no time or change could heal.

Some six weeks passed uneventfully by, and then a strange thing happened which caused a slight ripple on the calm of the children's existence. One day the two little girls were going through the streets with an attendant when a dirty, ragged child of about four or five slipped away from a band of beggars and ran after the party.

"Save me! Save me! I am Little Small-Feet! I have been stolen and they beat me!" she cried.

They turned to see a grimy, dirty ragamuffin, clad in one thin garment, whose hollow eyes and scrawny hands no more resembled the Little Small-Feet they had known than the yellow cur at her heels looked like their well-cared-for Pekingese dog, and so they hurried away laughing. The beggar child ran crying after, until some one of the band of women noticed her absence and with a wild oath felled her to the ground and then, dragging her by the shoulder, pulled her down a narrow alley and disappeared.

On the children's return to their home, the first person they saw was Lord Chang and with great excitement they told their story to him. To their surprise he was very angry and said that he would have all the beggars beaten and driven out of town; he would not suffer his children to be insulted in such a manner. He warned them not to tell their mother what had happened for she would fret and that would make matters worse. The next day he went to the yamen and it was arranged that until further notice all beggars should be banished from the city.

A few days later Lord Chang received the official advancement which he had long sought. This time, he decided, his family should accompany him, for as viceroy of a large province he wanted the prestige a wife and children would give him. Before the Chinese New Year was celebrated with firecrackers and bonfires, the Changs had left the halls of their fathers and had set sail for a new province. Lord Chang left his little desired daughter behind him without a qualm, but he was careful to see that his ancestral tablets were packed with proper reverence and accompanied him on his journey.

Lady Chang was very sad as she stepped on board the stately junk that was to bear them away and her eyes filled with tears as she looked her last on the city. When the sails were spread and the anchor shipped, and she felt the swift current against the bow, she gave one glance at the muddy water, which she believed had swept away her darling and hurried to her cabin to weep, and the faithful Wang Dah Mah pushed back the other women when they would have crowded after, saying, "Leave our lady alone, for her heart must indeed eat bitterness to-night."

Alas for Little Small-Feet! The weeks that had brought such a desirable change in the fortunes of her father had brought a far different doom to her. Day after day of leaden misery dragged along until the child became almost stupid with fear and grief. The morning after the storm she had opened her eyes on a world which was a great contrast to anything she had ever known, and she began to scream with terror. But it did not take long for the girl to realize that if she wished to live at all, she must never make an outcry of any kind, for every sob was answered with a blow. Not long after sunrise Old Scarred Face appeared, and of all her tormentors Little Small-Feet early learned to dread her the most. The preceding evening her gay little garments had been taken off and she had been clothed in a filthy apology for a coat, and in the morning the waif's disguise was rendered all the more complete by the woman's smearing her with mud from head to foot.

After she had eaten rice from a broken bowl, Old Scarred Face took her by the hand and told the little one that she was to be taken back to her parents. Joyfully the child started out; her troubles were at an end at last. But after an hour's walk Little Small-Feet's hopes began to wane. Surely her home was not so many li away! Her weary footsteps began to drag. This slow pace did not suit the woman and she would jerk the little one's hand and pull her along, unmercifully expecting the child to keep step with her long stride. At length in a dirty alley they stopped before the door of a stable. After looking anxiously around for a moment, to see that they were not observed, Old Scarred Face entered. On one side of the stable was a pile of straw; this the beggar woman pulled aside, revealing the entrance to a half-lighted passageway. Having replaced the straw, the hag resumed her journey.

"If you ever speak of this place to a living person, I will pull your eyes out from the sockets and drag your tongue out by the roots," she threatened.

The weary journey was now at an end and they stood before the same iron door where the woman had waited on the preceding evening. Again the dwarf admitted her and they entered the presence of Creeping Sin.

The little shrinking creature thought that she had hated Old Scarred Face, but when she saw the leering smile of Creeping Sin she hid her face in the woman's coat and refused to look up until the beggar had dragged her forward.

Creeping Sin could not repress a chuckle to see the daughter of the haughty Chang in such disguise. "It's worth the whole ransom to see her thus," he said. "But now," turning to the beggar, "you may leave her clothes and go. When the moon comes to its first quarter, return, and I will tell you the result of my bargains. It will take at least that time to put them through."

"Slowly, slowly speak! you take too much upon yourself. The clothes," and she touched a bundle under her arm as she spoke, "I pawn until they are needed; if the brat appears in them before your servants they will show at once who she is, for a full description is in the mouth of all on the street."

"My servants are safe enough; not a single one but I have in my power and they know and are afraid. But as for the pawnbroker, he would sell his soul to the highest bidder. Give those clothes to me!" There was an almost mesmeric power in his eye that cowed the bold woman, the same power which the snake uses over the toad, so with only a moment's hesitation she laid the bundle on the table.

All through this conversation, Little Small-Feet had cowered against the wall, watching with terrible fascination the scene before her. The dwarf, the witch, or Creeping Sin—it would be hard to say which terrified her the most.

Old Scarred Face turned to go and taking the child by the shoulder, she gave her a shake, "Remember always what I have told you; if you ever speak of this to a living person or breathe it to a dog, I will do as I said and pull your eyes out from their sockets and drag your tongue out by the roots."

"And I," continued Creeping Sin as the door closed behind the woman, "will take your heart out and grind it to powder." Then turning to the dwarf, "Come, come, take the brat to Lui Sao Tze; she is expecting her."

The thought of being touched by the dwarf was too much for the suffering little one, and she fell unconscious at their feet.

When she finally came to herself the child thought for a happy moment that she had returned to her own home. The apartment was spacious and orderly, with all the marks that taste and wealth can give, and a woman whom she took for her amah was bathing her forehead. "O Wang Dah Mah!" she exclaimed; "I have had such a terrible dream!"

"This is not a place where dreams are made, unless it be nightmares," answered the woman with a harsh laugh.

"But where am I?" the child pleaded.

"In the same plight as the rest of us," the woman answered, "and we call it the Spider's den."

"Is the sly man the Spider?" asked Little Small-Feet eagerly, and the woman nodded assent, and told her to be careful for the walls had ears. The child was puzzled by this, but if it had anything to do with the man she had seen, she felt that the quieter she kept the better.

The days that followed were not so hard for Little Small-Feet. It is true, she longed for Wang Dah Mah's loving arms and quaint stories, and would cry herself to sleep each night because she felt so strange. But the woman was not unkind; the child had the clothes and food to which she was accustomed; and life did not seem very different from the home from which she had wandered. Creeping Sin was busy with more engrossing matters and had no time for one little stray more or less. Once he met her in the court yard and watched her with a crafty smile, because, on seeing him, she screamed and tried to run away

"You'll never forget me, will you, little Pearl?" he asked.

"No, I think not," faltered the child. The words must have been prophetic, for as long as Little Small-Feet lived, she remembered that scene and the horror she felt of this wicked man.

As years went by and her early home became a dim memory, the names of her parents were lost, and even the blue pagoda was surrounded by a haze, but Creeping Sin and his malignant face haunted her forever.

One beautiful autumn evening, the dwarf appeared at the door of the apartment where Little Small-Feet was and told her attendant that he was sent to take the child to his master.

With a cry the little one threw herself at the woman's feet and asked her to come too; she could not go alone for she knew that he would kill her. It was all in vain; the woman simply dared not intrude on her master without being summoned and the child was forced to follow her uncouth guide.

In the same room where she had first beheld Creeping Sin, she found him and her other tormentor, Old Scarred Face. They were both flushed and angry, and the hostile glances they cast upon the terrified waif would have frightened a much older person.

"True to his reputation," said Creeping Sin, the man has refused to listen to a word. He said that not a single cash would he pay. He never wanted another girl and this would save him the expense of rearing her, but if ever he met with those who stole his daughter, they would hang as high as the city gate. The whole thing had cost him all the time and trouble he was going to spend."

"But what are we to do with the brat?" asked Old Scarred Face.

"Oh, she's your 'thousand ounces of gold.' You found her; you can keep her. If she were older I might help you, for she has possibilities look at her hands and feet. But there are too many years ahead. As for the man, her father, we'll not forget what we owe him. Now you can go; I have wasted enough time over an unprofitable business."

Old Scarred Face was in two minds about a fit of passion, but feeling that it would avail her nothing, she caught at Little Small-Feet's hand and dragged her from the presence of Creeping Sin.

Then began a dreadful time for the delicately reared child; how she survived it for even one month will never be known. Who can describe Little Small-Feet's agony of mind when she followed her sisters one day and they failed to recognize her; or her horror when the order was given for the beggars to leave the city and she knew that she was leaving all hope behind when she cast her last look on her old friend, the blue pagoda? Perhaps the waif did not realize it, for she was barely five, and who can know the thoughts of a young child's heart?

Thus Little Small-Feet's life of wandering began; she was taken from city to city, through winter's cold and summer's heat, through deep mountain passes where wild beasts lurked, and in the huge cities on the plain where the human beasts are yet more savage. Always famished, ill-treated, and half-clad, she forgot her past and could look forward to no future, for each moment was one of grinding poverty that cut off all horizons. She was dead to the sufferings of the many children about her because all thought for any but herself had been taken from her.

From thousands of childhoods such as hers, men turn away their heads because they do not choose to see; but wilt not thou be pitiful, O God?

# Chapter IV

# The City That Lies in the Shadow of Purple Mountain

> There when the dim blue daylight lingers
>     Listening, and the West grows holy,
> Singers crouch with long white fingers
>     Floating over the zithern slowly:
> Paper lamps with a peachy bloom
>     Burn above on the dim blue bough,
> While the zitherns gild the gloom
>     With curious music! I hear it now!
>
> —Alfred Noyes.

Gentle Spring was again abroad on the road, traveling northward accompanied by her usual bodyguard of wayward breezes. Not long had she been at work, but traces of her magic could be' seen in tiny leaf buds and in the shimmer of green in the grasses of the hollows. The frogs in the ponds knew it, and were croaking lustily under the impression they were singing oratorios, while the birds were warbling in the tangled coppice. There was no doubt about it, hope was in the air!

Many li to the north of the City of the Blue Pagoda is situated the City That Lies in the Shadow of Purple Mountain. Very famous is this place and full of historic ruins; rebellions and revolutions have swept over it; dynasties have ruled and declined, until now its ancient grandeur has fallen to decay.

This March evening the setting sun had cast a glorious garment of lavender and gold over the city, as if to cover with an emperor's cloak the signs of destruction and the marks of time. Soft, pink clouds still lingered around the summit of Purple Mountain as if loath to say good night, and the winds that arise at twilight had begun to whisper in the trees. The City That Lies in the Shadow of Purple Mountain was sprawled, like a huge dragon, on the plain below. A few scattered huts reached almost to the mountain's foot, while the suburbs extended out side the wall with more or less density of population to the banks of the mighty, hurrying river ten miles distant. The streets hummed with the usual noise of hawkers calling their wares, dogs barking, women screaming to their neighbors, and coolies uttering the peculiar singsong whereby they seek to make their burdens lighter; because the sun was setting with unusual splendor was no reason why they should lay down their tasks; the hush of nature was nothing to them!

A little to one side, where the population was less congested and there was room for breathing space, arose the gray walls of the foreign hospital, shaded by trees and surrounded by the restful green of lawns and the gay colors of yellow daffodils and crocuses. The people of the city held this place in awe, for there were many dark rumors of what went on within its walls. Stories were circulated of babies ground to powder and of horrid rites and sorceries, and as they spread, the wonder of them grew and also the terror of the hospital.

In the window of a ward stood a young woman in nurse's uniform, whose sad eyes were fixed on the fading glory which brought back happy memories of her far-away country.

"If it were not for Purple Mountain and these evening lights I do not believe that I could stand the sordidness and misery," she thought. "I would just have to leave it and sail for home."

She watched the bright glow fade and the recesses fill with the purple shadows for which the mountain was named, and then greatly heartened and with her usual shining look she returned to her interrupted duties.

Beautiful as it appeared in the evening light, all was not well on Purple Mountain. If the recesses and caves could have spoken, they might have told many a tale of crime and horror scarcely fit for gentle ears, for in one of the very crevices that the nurse had watched was settled a human brood whose existence was scarcely higher than that of the pariah dogs that roamed the streets stealing and quarreling. These people are the "beggars" who belong to a close fraternity; the house dogs are taught to bark at them and drive them from the door; the charitable drop an occasional cash into their outstretched bowls, and by these means and by petty thieving they subsist—unless, like Old Scarred Face, they have a head for schemes and plots and can thus make a more profitable livelihood. Their dwelling place in this instance was a cave formed by a cleft in the rocks, the only light being that afforded by a smoldering fire of reeds over which some primitive cooking was done. The air was thick with smoke and heavy with vile odors, while the language of the men and women was dreadful to hear.

On a heap of dirty straw in one corner lay a child evidently in pain, for every now and then she uttered a low moan. She was a mass of rags and filth; her unkempt hair had apparently never known a comb; the only feature that showed through the grime was a pair of dark eyes, bright with fever.

Squatted on the floor near her were two crones, who might have sat for portraits of the Fates and Furies: their scant hair stood out in wisps; almost all of their teeth were gone and their red gums had a horrid, bestial look; their thin hands were like the claws of birds; their padded garments were so tattered that it seemed a marvel that they did not fall from their bony shoulders.

Absolutely regardless of the child that lay so near, they coolly discussed her fate. The older woman, whose face was marked by smallpox, was speaking.

"You talk foolishly. It is useless to feed the brat longer. Now that her leg is so bad that she cannot go out with me and beg, she is not worth a string of cash. Little did I think, when I took her from the noble family that lives to the south, that they possessed so many daughters that they would not feel it worth while to pay me a ransom. She was handsomely dressed, too, but the rascally pawnbroker gave me a mere song for her clothes, and I did not dare demand more for fear that he would squeal. When I burned her leg and rubbed dirt into it, I thought that I had done a clever trick for I told people that she had been bitten by a serpent and they paid to see the sore, so it worked well for a season. But the child is no use this way. If the gods will that she should die I will not burn incense to keep her alive," and she cackled harshly at the joke.

"Why don't you take her down to the foreign hospital?" suggested the other woman, in whom there was a little spark of humanity left. "They would take her in and make her well to boot. You know, Old Scarred Face, they would not charge anything."

"Yes, and a pretty story she would tell of the way she has been treated! Those foreigners are silly about children and make a horrid fuss when they think the 'torments' have been abused. She is not worth the trouble and has cost me far too much already."

The two women moved away to get their share of rice, leaving poor Little Small-Feet—for alas! this is what she had come to—shivering and terror-stricken in the corner. Did ever the little breezes play a sorrier trick than on the day they tempted Little Small-Feet to visit the blue pagoda?

As she lay on the floor, the waif could have screamed at the thought of being left to starve, but knowing that her cries would mean a beating she only lay and moaned.

In a few minutes the kindlier of the two women came and held a bowl of weak tea to the child's lips and slipped into the feverish fingers a small portion of bread. It was the first food Little Small-Feet had tasted that day and she gulped it down eagerly. She knew however, that this relief was only temporary, for the woman was starting south in the morning and then what her fate would be, she hardly dared think.

Over three years had passed since Little Small-Feet had been stolen—years that are better forgotten. The scars of stripes on her back and the hunted look in her eyes alone would tell a story, and now at length the end had come to this miserable existence, or so it seemed to her. Still the words that she had heard rang in her ears. Could it be possible that at the hospital she might find a refuge? It would not be worse than dying here of starvation. She remembered the hospital and where it stood; many times she had passed it. How could she ever reach the place when it lay so far away? Then she thought of the pilgrims she had seen crawling on their sides to holy shrines, in order to acquire merit. Surely she could do as much to save her life! The beggars by this time were fast asleep; now was her chance; she must get away from the path that led to the cave before dawn, if she did not want to be brought back and certainly killed.

So once again Little Small-Feet decided to run away, but this time there was no glee or joy in her heart, only a bitter, bitter fear. With the strength of desperation she crept out of the stuffy cavern, and as the cool night breezes blew across her face, her courage strengthened. Surely the little breezes could not recognize their one-time playmate in such a guise, yet they did her a friendly deed to keep her company to-night. Like a great human caterpillar she edged her way along the stony path; brambles caught at her face and tore her hair like tiny elfin hands holding her back; toads and insects slipped between her fingers; and once a snake glided out from under a stone into the brush on the other side of the road.

Frightened as she was of all these creatures, they were not half so terrible as the human creatures she had left behind, so she crept steadily on, and as the first faint streak of dawn brightened the eastern sky and flushed the sides of Purple Mountain, she turned into a side road far enough away from the cavern to escape the fear of detection. Nevertheless each moment seemed fraught with some terror; sometimes it would be the sight of a beggar in the distance, when she would lie on her face or crawl under the shadow of a wall; again some fierce dog or half-wild pig would come up and menace her with its sharp teeth. The passers-by paid little heed to the wanderer; they were accustomed to the sight of misery and one child more or less did not count.

When the afternoon was waning, Little Small-Feet was still a long distance from her destination and her strength was failing so fast that she began to despair of reaching the hospital that night. In that case she felt that she would never live until the morning, for the dogs and pigs would be bolder at night, as they were fierce with hunger.

At last, with courage utterly gone, she began to cry and a passing countryman heard the sound coming from what he at first supposed to be a bundle of rags. He had plenty of time, so he stopped his creaking wheelbarrow and stooped over the little refugee.

"What is the matter here?" he asked in a friendly voice. "We do not need your tears to water the ground; we have moisture enough with out that as the gods of the floods will tell you." For a moment he received no answer, but after a short coaxing Little Small-Feet explained her trouble. Perhaps the rough farmer had a daughter at home, for he told the weeping child to cease crying and as he happened to be going in the direction of the city he would take her as a passenger.

The clumsy wheelbarrow was no swift-moving ambulance, and every turn of the wheel was torture to the injured child, but Little Small-Feet bore it with the stoicism learned from hard usage. The thought that she would certainly reach the hospital before dark had completely restored her courage.

"I must leave you here," the countryman announced when they had come within a few doors of their destination. "It is all very well for you to risk having the foreigners cast the evil eye upon you. You have nothing to lose, but with me it is different. I have a pig and some chickens, and I could not afford to have them die," and he hurried away for fear he might meet the outlandish strangers.

The waif crawled painfully to the hospital gate and settled herself on the threshold, for she had no strength to knock. She was haunted indeed by the dread that her painful journey might be in vain and that she might be refused admission.

Fortunately Little Small-Feet had not long to wait, for soon she heard a voice talking in unfamiliar accent on the other side of the gate; the hinges creaked and a tall form almost trod on her as she lay. There was an exclamation of surprise and then she was gently lifted and carried up the garden walk to the hospital. For the first time in three bitter years Little Small-Feet felt a touch that was not hostile, and instinctively she knew that she was safe.

On entering the hospital they turned immediately into the reception room and she heard her new-found friend say words that sounded beautiful to her ears.

"Well, Miss Faith, here is another little waif for you to mother."

Then at last Little Small-Feet dared to open her eyes and she looked up into the very kindest, sweetest face she had ever seen. The light, curly hair, eyes the color of the skies, and aquiline nose, looked very odd and outlandish, and the little one wondered why she was not afraid, but instead she relaxed into the arms outstretched to take her with a sigh of deep content.

With never a doubt or shrinking the nurse held her burden, but tears sprang to her eyes and ran unheeded down her face as she noticed the sign of abuse and neglect so plainly visible; she wondered how many more such children wandered the streets of the city.

The doctor, having put his charge in the proper care, delayed long enough to ask her name.

"My name is Little Small-Feet," the child answered wearily.

"That is a very honorable name," he replied, "but you must have another; try to think!"

"Nothing else, only Little Small-Feet," she answered.

"But your parents—what are they called?"

"I suppose I had a father and mother—indeed Old Scarred Face told the other woman so—but they did not want me; I was only a girl, you know, and I lost them so long ago that I do not remember."

Seeing that the matter was hopeless, the doctor dropped it for a season and started on his rounds. Little Small-Feet then underwent an experience that terrified her more than all the ill-usage she had ever had, for she did not know what it meant; and she wondered if, after all, it might not be preliminary to being ground to powder. Her clothes were taken away from her and she was given a bath. It was a long and thorough process, and through it all Little Small-Feet gave vent to the screams and cries that had been pent up in her small body through years of misuse. When it was finally over and she was laid in a clean bed, nurse and patient were both exhausted, and Little Small-Feet fell immediately into a restful sleep.

Gentle Spring arose with the sun the next morning, and gave direction to her friends that of all of the days of the year this was to be the sweetest, for a tired child had found shelter. So when Little Small-Feet opened her eyes, a soft breeze was wandering in and out of the window by her cot, waiting to speed and tell the others that the child was awake and they must be on the alert. Then he flew to a bed of violets, and gathering an armful of fragrance, he hurried back through the window, only stopping long enough in the shrubbery to warn the birds that now they must sing as they had never sung in all their life before. The song of the birds, the fragrance of the violets, and the soft comfort of her bed quite bewildered Little Small-Feet, for the moment. What was the strange room with its windows and doors, and its rows of beds, and how had she come here? Then suddenly the recollection of yesterday and her flight came over her; this was the hospital, and all this foreign sorcery. Had they changed her, too, she wondered, into the likeness of a fox or some other animal? The waif held up her bony hand; no, it looked the same as ever, only infinitely cleaner!

As far as that was concerned everything was clean; the floors the walls, the beds all seemed to gleam. She had never known anything like it, but how comfortable it was! Would Old Scarred Face dare look for her here? At the thought the child hid herself beneath the covers. But soon she heard a footstep and peeped out to see standing before her the new-found friend holding a steaming bowl of soup. The light in the stranger's eyes, the tender smile on her lips, and the cadence of her low voice must have been some strange magic, for at that moment she stole the heart of Little Small-Feet. There were many painful dressings to undergo, but she bore them much better than she did the surprising bath. As hour followed hour and she lay quite still, her face was always turned toward the door through which the nurse entered. When the child saw that her friend was coming at last, her whole expression would change and it would be hard to recognize her as the same dull little figure that was found on the doorstep that March evening. So the nurse would linger by the bed, telling stories of her home across the sea and all sorts of facts and fancies, just for the sake of seeing the smile that chased away the shadow from the little one's face.

"Your name may be Miss Faith, but I call you my Great Helpful Lady!" said Little Small-Feet one day as she patted her friend's hands with those long, slender fingers that seemed to prove her gentle birth. From that moment the child refused to use any other name.

Time flew fast in the hospital that spring; the cheer that came from the merry song of the birds in the compound trees seemed to be reflected in all the wards, and there was no sunnier, happier place to be found than around Little Small-

Feet's bed. At first her language was dreadfully coarse, and her manners and habits appalling, but as she associated more and more with the Great Helpful Lady, these coarse ways gradually dropped away, and in this more refined atmosphere she returned unconsciously to the courteous customs she had learned in her own home.

A morning came at length when she was wrapped in a warm rug and carried out into the garden. May was in the air and all the paths were gay with flowers. Little Small-Feet clapped her hands with joy at the riot of color and settled herself back with a sigh of content in the comfortable chair.

"O Little Small-Feet, I forgot the very nicest thing of all," explained her friend and hurried away to return in a minute with a knobby bundle in her hands. She gave it to the child saying, "This came all the way from 'the City by the Sea' particularly for you."

With eager, trembling fingers Little Small-Feet undid the strings and before her bewildered eyes appeared a lovely little foreign doll. She gave a cry of joy and hugged it close, and then turned to her friend such a look of adoring homage, that the giver could scarcely refrain from tears; but she laughed instead and said: "This baby will bear you company when I am away from you, won't she? Now I must run away to my other children."

When the Great Helpful Lady returned an hour or two later, the child was so absorbed that she did not hear her step on the soft turf. The new doll was clasped tightly in its mother's arms and she was gently croning over it these words:

> "The small-footed girl
>   With the sweet little smile,
> She loves to eat sugar
>   And sweets all the while.
> Her money's all gone
>   And because she can't buy,
> She holds her small feet
>   While she sits down to cry."

"Why, Little Small-Feet," the lady exclaimed, "what a charming lullaby and all about yourself, too! Where did you ever learn it?"

Little Small-Feet looked up startled. "I don't know because just as seem going to remember I suddenly forget, but I think her name was Wang Dah Mah."

"And who was Wang Dah Mah? Try hard to remember; it might help us to find your friends. Where did you see her and how long ago?"

"O my Great Helpful Lady, I cannot think! I have seen so many people and been in so many places, and the only faces I seem to remember are Old Scarred Face and Creeping Sin." As soon as she had mentioned these two names a great terror overcame the child; she began to weep and turned deadly pale, casting frightened glances behind her, as if half expecting to see her two enemies hovering near.

"O my Great Helpful Lady, do not let us speak of them, for I know they will kill me if they ever find out that I have told their names!"

Little Small-Feet seemed so overcome that the nurse felt it better to change the subject for the present. It was only bit by bit, when she held the child in her arms and the little one's arms were around her neck, and her mouth close up to the nurse's ear, that Little Small-Feet confided the story of her terrible wanderings. Very often the Great Helpful Lady lay awake until the small hours of the morning, her heart so oppressed with the stories she had heard that sleep refused to come.

No clue, however, was found to Little Small-Feet's family or the city from which she had roamed. The stay in the Spider's den had wiped out all recollection of what went before except such little things as the lullaby and Wang Dah Mah's name, which proved in the end no clue at all.

As the weeks went by the Great Helpful Lady grew more and more desirous of adopting the waif, but the hospital authorities felt that this would be unwise, for if it should get noised abroad that a beggar child had been adopted, the hospital would be overwhelmed with foundlings left by thousands of poor people, and there was neither funds nor space to keep such a number.

The nurse comforted herself, however, with the thought that she would find some kind native family and arrange with the family to care for the child.

Alas, for plans and dreams! Before Little Small-Feet was well enough to be moved from the hospital, the steaming months of July and August fell upon the city, and the Great Helpful Lady came down with malaria that always stalks the summer streets, and immediately she was ordered away to the mountains to save her life. Even in her fever the lady did not forget her favorite, and left many directions about her. But the hospital was short-handed during the hot season, and the staff terribly overworked, and in this condition Little Small-Feet's interests were overlooked. No one could tell exactly how it happened, but when the Great Helpful Lady returned in the autumn, she found that Little Small-Feet had been dismissed, leaving no trace behind.

The Great Helpful Lady was inconsolable; she instituted inquiries in every direction and when ever she went outside her gate she examined each child she met in the hope that it might prove to be her little friend. In her long walks she had the girl constantly on her mind, and twice she went as far as Purple Mountain and as she climbed its steep sides she marveled at the courage of the wanderer who had dared to crawl over such steep places with her wounded leg; and ever as she walked she called, "Little Small-Feet, Little Small-Feet!" But the reverberating echoes only mocked her, and wearied and disheartened she was forced to retrace her steps alone.

# Chapter V

# When Violets Came Again

> Hold by right and rule by fear
> Till the slowly broadening sphere
> Melting through the skies above
> Merge into the sphere of love.
>
> —Alfred Noyes.

Month followed month and the dreary, dark days of winter cast their gloom over the City That Lies in the Shadow of Purple Mountain. The rich put padded garment over padded garment and added a fur-lined coat thereto, thus challenging the cold to do its worst, and adding much to their girth and the importance with which they were regarded. The poor shivered in their rags and perished with want on the street corners and in their miserable huts, while the life of the city flowed relentlessly by them. At the hospital nothing was heard about Little Small-Feet; she had disappeared as completely as a pebble thrown into a pond. Only the winds moaning down the mountain side could have told of her whereabouts and their sharp tongues were too busy about other matters to give time to wandering beggar children. But the Great Helpful Lady often stopped in the midst of her duties to wipe away a tear at the thought of her favorite straying homeless in the bitter weather.

Winter winds gave way at length to softer breezes and spring brought hope and warmth to the shivering city. On one of these bright mornings the Great Helpful Lady was standing at the gatehouse talking with some friends. Suddenly she heard a cry and saw a pathetic bundle of rags come limping toward her; as she reached the lady the little girl stumbled and fell headlong; some instinct told the nurse who it was and she ran forward with an exclamation of pity. The child did not attempt to rise but lay there hugging her friend's feet, and the lady, stooping; gathered her up in her arms regardless of grime and dirt, fondling and crying over her, while Little Small-Feet kept repeating, "My Great Helpful Lady! My Great Helpful Lady!"

Could there be any doubt of the wanderer's fate after such a scene? The bystanders thought not and at once decided that by right of conquest the wayfarer belonged to the lady. This time the necessary bath was welcomed with glee, but it proved an even longer process than the famous first attempt, because Little Small-Feet interrupted it so often to stroke the hand that held the sponge.

Little Small-Feet's terror of Old Scarred Face had grown and trebled in the past few months, and it was with much difficulty that she was coaxed to tell her story. The lady gathered that the beggar was lying in wait for the child when she was dismissed from the hospital, and immediately seized her and stripped off her clothes, and nearly naked, the poor little victim had been forced to return to the old life of terror. Old Scarred Face had again burned the waif's leg, and she had been kept a prisoner in the cave, but one day when she had been left alone by mistake, Little Small-Feet escaped and dragged her way back to her protectress.

"Do you know, my lady, one day before the winter fell, I was in the cave and I thought I heard your voice calling me, 'Little Small-Feet, Little Small-Feet,' and I ran to the mouth of the cave and tried to answer, but Old Scarred Face knocked me down and said that should you come for me, all the beggars would kill you, so I did not dare to answer again."

"Yes, it was I, Little Small-Feet, out on the mountain calling for you," said the lady.

"I am so glad that you did not forget me, but I wish Old Scarred Face would; I am afraid she never will. I think Creeping Sin is here, too, for one of the children told me that he and the woman met in the city, and I think he is worse than Old Scarred Face."

A beautiful new day now dawned for Little Small-Feet. To be surrounded by love, to be assured that she would never again be parted from her friend—these things conspired to bring the light back into her face. The only cloud, and that indeed heavy, was the thought of Old Scarred Face hovering like some bird of prey ready to pounce, if for a minute Little Small-Feet should be found alone. It wrought such terror in her childish mind that often in the night she would awaken with a scream. Then her friend would hurry to her side with a light in her hand, and the patients in the ward would bless the shadow as she passed of this second "lady of the lamp."

When the sun peeped in through the window, all Little Small-Feet's terror would fly away and her merry laugh would ring out through the corridors, the fears that lurked in the darkness quite forgotten. She constituted herself the tutor of the other little children in the ward, and there was nothing she liked better than to lead the tots by the hand through the hospital and explain to them the queer ways of the strangers from beyond the seas. One lovely afternoon, Little Small-Feet was seen guiding a small cripple carefully down the ward, and in their progress they paused for a brief moment below a print of Christ blessing the children.

"And who is this 'heaven-born man'?" the lame boy asked in an awed whisper, pointing upward to the picture.

"I do not know very much about him yet, for I am very stupid," hesitated the girl, "but he is a friend of my Great Helpful Lady, because she told me so, and you can see that he must be, for he holds the little ones in his arms with a great love in his face, just the way my lady does the hospital babies." Then perfectly satisfied they resumed their halting journey.

That evening when the nurse went to bid Little Small-Feet good-night she found her weeping grievously.

"Why, Little Small-Feet, what in the world is the matter?" inquired her friend in some alarm.

"O my Great Helpful Lady, I am eating bitterness and my heart is not at rest because of all of the little children out in the streets with no one to care for them. When I was with them I did not know children ever were happy, and I was so miserable myself that I did not care. But now sometimes when I am at play and think of those children, I feel that I can never smile again."

"Ah, Little Small-Feet, we need your smile here of all places; it is your part to make the sad people gay. Perhaps some day you will tell me more about the children and we can think of a way to help them."

"Well, I have thought of one thing but it sounds foolish for a little girl; I should like to study very, very hard and learn to be a doctor; then perhaps I could make people well the way you do. I could go out in the streets and look for beggar children, for I know all their haunts, and I could make them well and happy, too."

"Why, what a nice idea!" exclaimed her friend, "I will certainly try to help you by seeing that you have the best education a woman can receive. You shall study in my own country and afterwards you can come back and we will work together." Then she laughed: "What castles in the air we have been building when you should have been asleep. There are many streams to cross and oceans, too, before they can come true. But the only way to make dreams really happen is to be willing to sacrifice everything for them, our pleasures, our time, and our comfort. So good-night, little schemer, and in the morning we will see what we can do."

Early next day when the nurse stopped for a moment before an open window, and was drinking in the scent of the lilacs, she heard Little Small-Feet's voice and, turning suddenly, found the child making deep ceremonial bows before her—the bows that Old Wang Dah Mah had taught her in those happy days so long forgotten.

"Well, dear little Peach Blossom," said her friend, "what is it now?"

"O gracious lady, may I go to school and learn to read? Pao Tse[1] is much smaller than I and she can recognize many characters, and she knows the 'Girl's Classic' by heart, and Tien Sih[1] too has learned the 'Rules for the Behavior of Children,' and I can repeat them from hearing him say them so many times. You know, he is really very dull and it takes a long time to learn things"—and in a laughable imitation of Tien Sih's singsong, Little Small-Feet recited,

> "Awake with the morning, arise with the sun,
> Retire late at night when your lessons are done,
> Remember that age will come easily on,
> Utilize youth, it will quickly be gone."

"Well, small pleader, are there any more arguments?" asked her friend, smiling down into the eager, upturned face.

"Yes, yes. You remember about little Che Wu who lived hundreds of years ago? He was so eager to read that he learned by the pale moonlight reflected from the snow."

"There is no danger of Tien Sih's ruining his eyes in that manner at any rate," laughed the lady. "As for you I am glad that you want to learn, and I will teach you myself every day, for it is too late to begin school this year, as it will soon close for the summer, but when we are away in the mountains we ought to accomplish a great deal."

Little Small-Feet had never heard more delightful news, and she fairly danced with glee. The thought of being taught by her lady and that they were to go together to the mountains, was almost too much joy; it went to her head like wine, and she went to find some one to share in the good news.

---

[1] Pao Tse means Precious Thing. Tien Sih should be translated Heavenly Piety, though in this case, Earthly Mischief would have been far more appropriate.

As she ran out into the garden on whom should her eyes rest but Tien Sih, playing some fascinating game with ball and string. "O Tien Sih, Tien Sih," she called, "guess what beautiful thing is to happen?"

Tien Sih, though wild to know, assumed after the manner of his sex manly indifference. Alas, why do such tactics always prove successful?

"I am going to school and to the mountains with my gracious Helpful Lady," Little Small-Feet continued, longing for sympathy.

Instead of the sympathy she expected, a wave of jealousy struck like a dart through Tien Sih's masculine soul; no one had urged him to accompany them to the mountains; in fact the urging would have been all the other way.

"What's the use of going to school, when you are too big a coward to go to Sunday school with me?"

"You know I've been forbidden to go outside the compound without a grown-up person, and if you had ever seen Old Scarred Face you would be afraid, too."

"I am afraid of nothing, for I'm a man. I could kill a tiger or a wolf as easy—but you are a coward and a beggar, and you can never go to school without leaving the compound, so that is settled."

Little Small-Feet had plenty of temper of a very spicy brand, and to be called a beggar and a coward was adding insult to insult. In her wanderings she had learned to fight for her own protection and her companions had a decided respect for her prowess. She sprang at Tien Sih, who was not expecting such an onslaught, and never in his life before had the boy been so thoroughly punished. The little girl used all the approved methods of beggardom, tooth, nails, and feet, and Tien Sih soon fled before the tempest.

"You're afraid all the same, and a horrid beggar as well!" he called after her and hurried off to tell his father that Little Small-Feet was not a fit playmate for decent, well-brought-up boys like himself, of good family, too, whose father was cook of a prominent hospital and making such a fortune out of it.

Tien Sih's father told him plainly to hold his tongue about the fortune. "Think twice and say nothing," would be a fitting motto for him hereafter. However, the man was indignant that a beggar brat should have had the effrontery to treat any child of his with such indignity, and he started immediately for headquarters with his complaint.

Poor Little Small-Feet, brought up by an amah and then by Old Scarred Face, knew no resource in such a crisis but to make up a story. Alas, it did not hold water! There were too many witnesses, and so she stood convicted. Her Great Helpful Lady looked and talked in such a sorrowful manner that Little Small-Feet's heart was nearly broken and this taught her more than many punishments the necessity of truthfulness if she wished to please her friend.

The children, however, had not confessed to the cause of the quarrel and so the next Sunday when Tien Sih said, "If you are really sorry for fighting me you will go with me to Sunday school," Little Small-Feet decided that this was the only way to show her deep repentance, and consented to go. They watched until they saw the gatekeeper walk to the hospital on an errand, then they slipped out of the gate and started with stout hearts down the lane. They made their first turn safely and were happily engaged in talking about what they were about to see when a skinny arm, extended from behind a stone wall, clutched the all-unsuspecting Tien Sih by the queue. Very much astonished they turned to see before them a horrid-looking beggar woman, mouthing at them in triumph. Little Small-Feet's first instinct was to run, but she could not leave Tien Sih in Old Scarred Face's clutches, so made bold by fear, she flew at the woman screaming desperately for aid.

Help was not far away, for the hospital doctor had seen the children disappear through the gateway and had hurriedly followed them, and when Old Scarred Face heard footsteps behind her, she quickly fled.

This incident proved only too clearly Old Scarred Face's malice and from that day forward none of the children dared to venture out alone. As for Little Small-Feet, for many years her prayers ended: "Please don't let Old Scarred Face get me! Amen."

At length the July heat blew over the city like the hot breath of a dragon and the day arrived for the long-desired trip to the hills. Little Small-Feet had talked mountains, eaten mountains, and dreamed mountains for the past few weeks, but when the moment of departure finally arrived, the busy tongue was quiet; her joy was beyond all the powers of speech. The whole available population from the foreign concession was at the gate to see them off. Little Pao Tse and Tien Sih were there, green with very unheavenly envy, and the doctor, the nurses, and all the servants, down to the water coolies, crowded around to wish them a prosperous journey and a safe return.

As Little Small-Feet climbed to her place, she was the happiest child in the whole Middle Kingdom, but as they moved from the gates, she saw with horror, on the outskirts of the crowd of curious neighbors, the leering face of her old enemy. It was seven miles to the landing where they were to take the steamer, and their progress was necessarily slow, and half that distance Old Scarred Face followed them, reviling horribly, until at length the coolies drove her away. Poor Little Small-Feet was half dead with terror. It was a sad beginning, indeed, to the longed-for summer. The child had ceased to believe in malignant spirits but memories of old superstitions clung to her mind like cobwebs. Could it be possible that her dear lady was mistaken, after all, and that the mischievous beings were urging Old Scarred Face on, and laughing at Little Small-Feet up their sleeves all the time? She almost wished that she had done as Tien Sih had advised and put on a charm against the evil eye, for Tien Sih, although he attended Sunday school regularly, felt that it was wise to keep in favor with both sides.

The river steamers that ply the waters of the great empire are tied down to no fixed schedule; they arrive at any hour and depart when their cargo has been discharged. The traveler soon learns not to fret at delay, or murmur if he reaches the wharf and finds that the boat for that day has already departed. Little Small-Feet and her friend made themselves as comfortable as they could on the dirty hulk with coolies and hotel runners curled up and asleep in almost every available spot. The steamer was even later than usual and would not arrive for several hours. The heat grew more and more intense, while the odors from all sorts of merchandise seemed to stifle them. They moved from spot to spot in a vain attempt to find some air stirring, while their faithful amah sat as contemplatively as a Buddha, guarding their heap of luggage.

They had been waiting several hours when suddenly one of the men in charge of the wharf came running toward them.

"Quick! You must hide!" he exclaimed. "You are in grave danger here, follow me!" Without hesitation they followed him, as he led the way between high bales of goods reaching yards above their heads. It was dark and stifling, but on they went to the farthest end of the hulk, and there he showed them where they could creep under some loose straw that might perhaps hide them. He heaped some empty barrels around them, leaving at the lady's request a small peephole from which they could see down the river and watch for the approach of the boat.

"What has happened, and why do you hide us here?" the astonished lady exclaimed.

"A swift messenger has just arrived from the city, saying that an angry mob of beggars and riffraff are coming, and they swear they will kill you and take the child. They claim that you have stolen her for the sake of killing her, because you want her bones for medicine. Some of the city people have become alarmed and have joined in the riot."

"How does it happen that you care to save us?" whispered the nurse, "and where are amah and the boy?"

"Do you not remember me? My unworthy name is Meng, and I was cured at the hospital. I believe the doctrine and I can never forget your gracious kindness. If you stay here I think you will be safe, and I will tell the mob that they cannot enter the hulk unless they buy their tickets. I think that I can keep them until the boat comes. The amah and boy are Chinese and safe enough."

One man's loyalty alone lay between them and an awful fate. On what a slender thread their safety depended!

"Pray now, Little Small-Feet, if you have never prayed before!" softly whispered the lady in whose steady tones there was never a quaver.

"And are you suffering this danger for me, for me?" sobbed the child.

"There was One who suffered far more than this for me, little one!"

The distant clamor of the mob could soon be heard like the roar of surf beating against the rocks. The sound of running feet approached nearer and the cries of men and women out for blood, and as they became louder the cries were horrible.

"It's like the cry of the pack!" thought the lady.

The heat was suffocating, when suddenly a breeze that had been playing languidly around the wharf seemed to sense that an old friend needed succor, for running out over the water, it suddenly turned and, making little ripples on the current, blew gently across their hiding place and revived their fainting spirits.

The two refugees thus huddled together scarcely dared to breathe; would their protector be loyal or would terror turn him traitor? Then above the din of the mob sounded the shrill whistle of a steamer and the pant of an engine. The boat was coming at last! The crowd heard it, too, and tried to rush the hulk, but their friend stood steadfast.

"You will answer to the governor if you step across this plank. There are men here who know you and your names will be reported. There is Old Scarred Face, and Lord Chang is searching for her now, and he is not so far north but his arm can reach her."

These bold words frightened the leaders; they saw the boat drawing near and the faces of the foreign officers staring inquiringly from the deck. These men were undoubtedly armed and they would not hesitate to use their arms for the protection of the lady and a little girl. Such barbarians were reckless with weapons when it came to protecting women and children. The quicker they turned heel the better for them, and the crowd melted away like hoarfrost.

Kind hands assisted the trembling woman and half-fainting child to the deck. When they were safely in their cabin, the Great Helpful Lady leaned over the berth where Little Small-Feet lay weeping.

"Ah, my child, we know now what it means when it says, 'He will give his angels charge over thee, to keep thee in all thy ways,' and are not angels better than evil spirits, Little Small-Feet?" she asked with a radiant smile. And the thoughtful little breezes wandered away to do some other gentle deed in a breathless, panting city.

# Chapter VI
# Where the Hills Were Blue

> Satin sails in a crimson dawn
>     Over the silky silver sea;
> Purple veils of the dark withdrawn;
>     Heavens of pearl and porphyry;
> Purple and white in the morning light
>     Over the water the town we knew,
> In tiny state, like a willow-plate,
>     Shone, and behind it the hills were blue.
>
> —Alfred Noyes.

Over the great river the summer brooded. On the shore the sun poured down with fiery heat drawing up clouds of fine moisture, but the progress of the steamer made a refreshing breeze upon the deck that revived weary bodies. Here, at least, there was no danger from wandering mendicants; surely now Little Small-Feet could throw off the terror that had followed her, waking and sleeping, for so many months.

How different was this swift journey from the heartbreaking travels of former years, when foot sore and weary the waif had been dragged from town to town, and her life had been one long round of misery! For two days the shores slipped by in a never-ending pageant and on the morning of the third, around a curve in the river, in the early sunrise, they saw the town where they were to disembark, and behind it, like the background of a screen, the hills rose, blue and amethyst.

Of course, there was a long delay before the steamer was finally fastened to the hulk and the gangplank lowered, and an endless parley with quarreling coolies before they could climb into their chairs and feel that the last lap of their trip was now before them. But at length they were off, through the tortuous streets and under the gateway in the great city wall, then out on the plains with the hot, hazy clouds above, and the tiny fields like a patchwork quilt around them. The paths were elevated above the surrounding country which lay ankle deep in water. Oh, the green of the rice as it simmered in the sun, and the purple mountains in the background, as they rose wave on wave from the foothills at their feet!

After swinging for an hour or two past tiny villages and endless laborers tilling their crops, the character of the country began to change. The ground became more broken and the path began to ascend, and as they ascended the beauty grew at every step of the way. Into cuplike valleys they went where cool streams tinkled, and the lush grass grew deep with lilies and other wild flowers. Higher still, their road edged precipices and a false step would have hurled them thousands of feet into some unseen torrent. Sometimes the path would be nothing but a series of roughhewn steps, up which their coolies would bear them as lightly as if they had been thistle down. And the summit, at sunset, when all the valleys were filled with changing, opalescent light, and far, far below the mighty river wound its way through the plain, looking like a thread of gold in a sea of pink and lavender!

"O my Great Helpful Lady, I never dreamed that any place in the world could be half so beautiful as this," cried Little Small-Feet. "I do not think even Old Scarred Face could be wicked here, but," she added wistfully, "I am afraid she has lost the habit of being good."

As if to make amends for the past roughness of her life, the summer months treated Little Small-Feet very gently. The days were fierce with heat, but every evening fresh breezes wandered down the valley and cooled the bungalows that lay in the shadow of the mountains. The summer showers seemed to beat with less fury than usual, and for whole days at a time they had no rain at all. In spite of picnics and hours spent in the open air, Little Small-Feet had to be conducted along the thorny road to knowledge, so a certain part of each day was set aside for study. Could it have been that her decided aptitude for learning was inherited from ancestors who boasted there had been scholars in the family as far back as the sage Confucius? One never knows but, if so, it was a help she did not realize; Little Small-Feet only bemoaned the fact that she had been born a stupid girl, for the taunts of Old Scarred Face and the imp, Tien Sih, were not forgotten.

"Why, Little Small-Feet, Old Scarred Face is a woman herself. I do not see why you care about what she said; I am a woman, too, and do you think me so outrageously dull?" asked her friend one day after the child had remarked, "I wish I had been born a boy."

"You are everything that is wonderful!" the girl answered. "But if I had been born a boy, my parents would have tried to get me back when I was stolen; being only a girl I was not desired."

When Autumn with her artist's colors had begun to turn their mountain top to red and gold, the friends knew that there must be no more dallying on these mountain paths and by the still river pools, even though their charm seemed to grow day by day more potent. There was a city lying on the plain whose cry rang in their ears, and the lady knew that she was one of the few who had the mystic touch that could bring peace and healing there.

"Are there not many nurses and doctors in your so great and noble country?" asked Little Small-Feet the last day before their departure.

"Yes, Little Small-Feet, many, many hundreds," her friend replied, as she thought of the number of doctors' signs on one street of an Occidental city, and the countless nurses sitting in their rooms waiting in vain for a possible case.

"Well, I should think, if they really studied to be nurses and doctors for the sake of making people well, they would try to go where the need was greatest and they could help most people. I know I would."

"Ah, little one, some do not know about the need here; indeed, I believe the majority of them do not. They are woefully ignorant of anything that happens outside the border of their own town. You must remember, too, that it takes a great amount of pity for others to make men turn their backs on comforts and home and go to a strange, hostile country that does not want them because it does not understand their motives. Homesickness is a terrible thing to fight and one must have a big vision to be able to leave friends for strangers one has never seen."

"Oh, my lady, are you so sorry, then, that you came?"

"Not for a moment; a person who has seen the suffering could never regret any sacrifice. Why, you alone make me glad."

"Yes, I should be dead by now if you had not come."

"Little Small-Feet, if Old Scarred Face were dying of some ailment you could cure, would you try to save her or would you let her die?"

The child hesitated, for this question was wholly unexpected. "I do not know," she answered bravely. "Of course you would, but then you do not know Old Scarred Face. If I did cure her, I would see that she was put into some place where she could do no more harm to little children."

"So would I," said her friend. "Fortunately we shall probably never be put to the test."

The next day with sober faces they turned the key on the little bungalow that had sheltered them all summer and again trusted their lives and their possessions to the hands of the coolies. The return journey was made uneventfully but who will blame Little Small-Feet for casting many apprehensive glances on the shore, as their steamer slowly approached the hulk?

"Why do you tremble, little one, and look so pale?" asked her friend. "Old Scarred Face is at the other end of the kingdom by now. From what you tell me she has probably a great many more important things to attend to than to watch one small girl from whom she can wring no money."

"You will never understand a person like Old Scarred Face, my lady. You would not be you if you could. She has beggars everywhere and they send word from mouth to mouth, telling what her enemies are doing. She never forgives anyone whom she thinks has wronged her, and she loves to torment them as a cat does a mouse. And," here the child whispered very softly, as if her slightest word would be borne by the wind to some unfriendly ear, "the dreadful part is, she always does manage to get the people in the end. What if she should get you, too? I never could bear it!"

"Don't forget the angels who are to take care of us, Little Small-Feet," answered the lady with a bright smile.

Whether Little Small-Feet was right or not, the first few months of their return were absolutely without alarm. The foreigners heard a rumor on the street that Old Scarred Face had been banished from the city on account of the riot, which had endangered some very delicate negotiations at the capital and had in consequence brought down official wrath on the ring leaders. The fact that some of the foreign governments were growing restless over the treatment given to their citizens in out-of-the-way places kept the official class on their good behavior, and the staff of the hospital felt more secure from insult than they had in years. Prejudice seemed to be melting, and here and there one could find a more enlightened person who would admit in a half-hearted way that there might after all be something good in the strange medicine and the new doctrine they had heard in the wards. These things all combined to lighten the air of dread in which Little Small-Feet lived. No precaution was omitted that was needed for her safety, but her life was freer and happier.

The irrepressible Tien Sih, too, began to feel that it might be to his advantage and to the advantage of his worthy father, the cook, to treat on almost equal terms the child who had basked all summer in the favor of the matron of the hospital. So he led the two little girls, Pao Tse and Little Small-Feet, into very much trouble first and last.

Then one bright morning in September another of Little Small-Feet's dreams came true. Before the sun had sent the tiniest shaft of gold into her room, the child was awake and dressing. Fondly she fingered her pretty, blue, grass-linen coat, and very neatly she adjusted each string and saw that it was tied in exactly the knot etiquette demands. Her shoes were a great source of pleasure, for she had made every stitch her self even to the stuffing of the quilted sole and she felt that her sewing would bear the closest examination.

"Now," she said to herself in triumph, "I am exactly like any other little girl!" There being no curly-headed Anglo-Saxon present to look surprised, this statement went unchallenged. Then she ran to her friend's room for a general inspection. "It seems as if all the country must be glad to-day!" the child exclaimed.

"If the people realized what the education of their girls is going to do for the nation, there would be bonfires and firecrackers set off all over this great city," answered her friend.

Holding tightly to the lady's hand, Little Small-Feet set off to school; her eyes sparkled and her feet would have danced but for the Girl's Classic, which had taught from the earliest times that a maiden should be dignified.

> "Let your laugh be never boisterous,
> Nor converse in noisy way,
> Lest your neighbors all about you hear whatever you may say;
> Then be dignified in walking, and be orderly in gait,
> Never lean against a doorpost, but in standing, stand up straight."

Soon they arrived at their destination and were properly introduced. When the teacher entered the classroom each girl rose in her place and gave her deep bow of respect to the most honorable lady, and then at last Little Small-Feet felt that she had left the rank of the beggars and could take her place among the scholars, and what a joy was hers!

The tiny god of mischief must have been jealous of such a quick road to success, for not more than a week had elapsed before trouble befell. The teacher was called away by a servant in the midst of one of the recitations; expecting to return in a minute, she ordered the girls to continue studying; but alas, scarcely was her back turned when a great noise arose in the street below!

"It's a wedding," exclaimed a girl. "The great official's daughter is to be married to-day."

Was there ever a woman anywhere who did not grow excited at the thought of a wedding? The window was high above their heads, placed there on purpose to prevent the girls from gazing out or from being seen by curious passers-by. Quick as thought, Little Small-Feet, to whom a great many of the rules of conduct for girls were unfamiliar, climbed on a bench and peered eagerly out of the window. There was a hush of consternation, then the other girls did the same, and when after five minutes the teacher returned, the pupils were all so absorbed that they did not hear her entrance. And after all it was not a wedding but a few wandering priests begging for alms and being roundly reviled by old Li Sao Tze because inadvertently they had upset a bucket of small fish standing at her door!

Punishment immediately followed. There was no doubt about the children's guilt; they had been caught in the act. Made wise by past experience, Little Small-Feet confessed her share and Pao Tze, fired by her brave example, did the same. The teacher was amazed; never in her whole career of teaching had a girl voluntarily admitted wrongdoing. She decided that it came from an unbecoming boldness on Little Small-Feet's part. In a twinkling she had sent the children home, with a note to their guardians.

Ah, if she could have seen the depths of Little Small-Feet's humiliation, she would have drawn some other conclusion. Pao Tze took it lightly, rather pleased than otherwise to have a holiday. But Little Small-Feet wept all day long and refused to eat or sleep, and in the evening she told her friend all about it.

"They will say that it was because I was a beggar child and will not want me in the school," she wailed. "My, why do I do wrong when I try so hard to be good?"

If only Wang Dah Mah had heard her, she would have shaken her head and said: "You are bound to be unlucky; you cannot fail to be. It is because the pagoda bells were silent at your birth; it was your parents' fault; they should have seen to it that the bells were rung!"

But the lady comforted her in other more practical ways, by suggesting that she study her native etiquette so that she should not again offend against the rules of good society. Little Small-Feet began to feel that obtaining an education was to cost more than she had dreamed, for it was not until her aptitude for study and her proficiency in games had put her at the head of the school that the girls stopped calling her "beggar child" and asking if she had seen a wedding lately.

Still another year slipped away, and another and another. In all this time no word was heard from Old Scarred Face and the fear of her gradually disappeared from the child's mind, so that she ceased to start and tremble at any sudden noise and to look apprehensively over her shoulder at the sound of a strange voice. The little girl was growing from a child into a sweet faced, low-voiced maiden. Sometimes in her expression there would be a wistful sadness as if she was looking at all the sorrow of all the world; at other times, however, she would be bright and gay; but, in whatever mood she was, she was very winsome and drew strangers irresistibly to her.

At length came a spring when the Great Helpful Lady was to return to her own land and take Little Small-Feet with her to be educated. Several weeks before they had planned to sail, the lady decided to give a birthday party for her favorite to celebrate the time when Little Small-Feet had first arrived at the hospital.

Now no little breezes whispered into Little Small-Feet's ear that she had ever had a birthday party before and she was just as excited as if it was her very first. As she had no recollection of that earlier occasion, this one seemed wonderful to her; nor did it worry her a bit that the highborn ladies in the City That Lies in the Shadow of Purple Mountain were absolutely oblivious of this social event. No coats and skirts stiff with embroidery were taken out and talked over for this festivity, and the caterers through out the town were not put to it to procure enough shark fins to suit polite palates.

Nor were costly presents worth almost a king's ransom prepared, but all the schoolgirls were stitching away in odd corners, full of haste to be prepared with a surprise for their friend when the auspicious day should arrive. For the girls' school and its teachers were invited and Tien Sih's father was very busy, hoping to establish his reputation forever. Tien Sih himself was for once full of regret over his masculine gender, for of course it would not be proper to have boys present—every parent would have protested in horror over such an idea. So Tien Sih could do nothing, but he took out his disappointment in making sarcastic remarks to his boy friends on the outlandish ways of foreigners, who were turning the world upside down and taking woman out of the sphere for which she was intended. Tien Sih at the age of fourteen was even more unbearable than he had been four years before the prosperity of his father, the cook, had certainly turned his head.

The hospital grounds had never looked so lovely as on the afternoon and evening of that soft spring day, and the garden was a bower of blossoms. Wonderful lanterns of every conceivable shape were hung in nooks and out-of-the-way corners, giving just the uncertain light that turns shrubbery and clumps of trees into fairy land. The tables were spread in the center of the lawn, and strings of lanterns above them added to the gayety of the scene. The girls in their soft blue and white coats were not unlike the flowers themselves, and the buildings rang with the music of happy voices.

Little Small-Feet's prosperity had sweetened and matured her in many ways and if Wang Dah Mah had seen her gentle, courteous greeting of every guest, she might have conceded at last that the spell wrought on the child by the silent pagoda bells had ceased to have effect. However that may be, it is a certain fact that had Little Small-Feet been told the story of her enchantment she would have heard it with a smile, for her dread of evil spirits had long ago fled.

"It's the evil in men's hearts that I am afraid of," she would say, with a shudder at the thought of her captivity.

Of all the people in the compound—not counting, of course, Little Small-Feet and her lady—the patients in the wards were the happiest that day, for at the girl's request each one received a bag of sweetmeats or a tiny gift, and early in the evening all the schoolgirls gathered beneath the hospital windows and sang their songs and glees.

It would take a ten-volume account to describe all the cheer and the good will at that party. Tien Sih himself, the sulky one, was not forgotten; besides, he and the whole cook's family, not to mention some of the neighbors, dined many days and well on the remnants. In the end Tien Sih quite reversed his opinion about the emancipation of women—for even in the Far East table dainties seem to be the most direct road to a man's affections.

In the midst of all these festivities the Great Helpful Lady disappeared. She was not missed at first for the fun was at its height, but when half an hour and then an hour slipped by, Little Small-Feet grew anxious.

"Ah, there she is!" all the girls exclaimed, when she at length came in sight, but only Little Small-Feet noticed that her friend seemed pale and absent-minded.

Even the happiest evenings come to an end, and the time finally arrived when all the guests must go and the fairy lanterns be blown out.

"Slowly, slowly, slowly walk," pleaded the polite hostess, when the girls made a motion to leave, "the time has been far too short." But in spite of protests and many delays they at length separated and Little Small-Feet and her guardian were alone.

Little Small-Feet urged her friend to retire, but the lady replied that she had a few things to see about and that the girl must not wait for her, and happy and tired the girl was soon fast asleep.

Then the lady began to do many strange things.

As soon as she was certain that her charge was unconscious she drew down the blinds so that not a crack of light could be seen; then she quietly took off her shoes, putting in their place a pair of noiseless slippers. This being done, she slipped to the door and opened it so suddenly that she nearly upset a man who was bent nearly double with his eye at the keyhole.

"Lao Wang, what are you doing here?" she sternly demanded. At that moment the doctor appeared at the other end of the corridor and she beckoned to him for help.

"This must be the man!" she exclaimed in English.

"Don't worry, I'll manage him," replied the doctor, seizing the man who had hoped to escape.

The nurse returned to her room, but this time she took the precaution to hang a rug over the door. Then, instead of preparing for bed, she continued her strange behavior. She pulled out a trunk from one corner and with great speed and caution as to noise, she began to fill it. Never was any trunk so quickly packed before and into it went all her own things and in a smaller one Little Small-Feet's precious possessions. It was nearly two o'clock before she had finished her task and a harder one lay before her: she must awaken a sleeping girl without being heard in the corridor.

"Little Small-Feet, Little Small-Feet," she whispered, "wake up, but be very quiet."

"Oh, what is the matter?" the girl sobbed, still drowsy and very much frightened.

"Old Scarred Face and Creeping Sin have returned, and are making a plot to burn all the foreign buildings and start a general riot. They have bribed Lao Wang, the coolie, to watch you and me so that they will be sure to catch us. The officials are now very unfriendly so they will not protect us. Their plans are not quite ready and if we can catch to-night's steamer, it may save the compound. All depends on our quietness; we were going soon and Old Scarred Face must have gotten wind of our plans."

"Didn't I tell you that she never forgets anybody?" Little Small-Feet shivered.

The cautions to be quiet were needless; quick as a flash the girl had caught the idea and, trembling and breathless, she soon dressed. A light knock was heard on the door; opening it on the crack they saw the doctor. He beckoned and they followed. The trunks must be left behind to be sent after them; they could take only a small bag with them, full of necessities.

Softly as shadows they slipped down the corridors and out to the back gate of the compound, which the doctor unlocked with the pass-key.

"Half an hour ago Lao Wang escaped," whispered the doctor to the lady as he assisted her into her ricksha; "the coolies are loyal; we will outrun them yet."

"Then this is a race with death?" she questioned.

Again the doctor nodded. "If the worst comes to the worst, we shall at least die together," he thought to himself.

"Quickly, very quickly!" he ordered the men and they started off at a brisk trot.

# Chapter VII

# Was It Creeping Sin?

> But, e'en as the moonlight air grew sweet,
> We heard the pad of stealthy feet
>    Dogging us down the thin white road;
> And the song grew weary again and harsh,
> And the black trees dripped like the fringe of a marsh,
>    And a laugh crept out like a shadowy toad;
> And we knew it was neither ghoul nor djinn:
> It was Creeping Sin! It was Creeping Sin!
>
>        —Alfred Noyes.

The night was full of lurking shadows which took on menacing shapes and seemed to threaten the fugitives with wild gestures as they approached, only to turn into harmless poles or trees when they reached them. A waning moon was half hidden by scurrying clouds, and its uncertain light made the shadows the more formidable. If only the pariah dogs could have taken the hurrying footsteps of the coolies as a matter of course, but at each group of houses they set up a howl as if to warn the householders that some dark deed was afoot. Even the roosters were in league against the little party and crowed so lustily and so often that they felt that the whole animal world was ready to turn and rend them.

Little Small-Feet sat erect, her hands clutching a bundle of treasures that she had hastily thrown together. Was this, then, to be the end of her and her dear lady, and were all their dreams for the future to be frustrated by the vengeance of her old enemies? It would have been better far to die in the cave on the mountain than to bring those who loved her into such peril. Suddenly she called to the coolies to stop, and the three rickshas drew up a stone's throw from some hovels.

"I am going back," she said to the doctor. "I cannot have you, my lady, run such risks for me. I will give myself up to Old Scarred Face. After all, it is I whom she wants, and if she once gets hold of me she will let you alone."

"O Little Small-Feet," exclaimed her friend, "do you understand us so little that you think we would ever allow it? Come, we must hurry on; each moment's delay is dangerous." And again the three took up their flight.

The eyes of the two women were fixed on the road in front, but the doctor, as he spurred the coolies on, frequently turned his head as he saw a low flicker of red rising over the city behind them. As he watched, the light grew brighter and shooting sparks went higher and higher. And he wondered to himself whether Old Scarred Face had accomplished her threat, and if the hospital was now in flames, what, then, had happened to the rest of the station?

As they drew nearer the river, down the wind came the sound of running footsteps, at first faint and hardly to be distinguished from the night wind in the willows, but soon plainer and yet more plain until the doubt became a certainty. Then the first faint flush of pink in the east gave promise of the dawn, but the eyes that were strained toward the river could not be lifted for one moment to see the hope of the morning, for before the sun rose in splendor, the race with death might be finished forever.

Now the voices of a crowd could be distinctly heard in the rear, coarse voices full of threatening, and around the bend in the road, the first of their pursuers might come at any moment. But joy, just ahead of the three rickshas was the turn that led to the wharf, and greater relief yet—at the hulk puffed and panted the steamer! The coolies, spurred to renewed efforts at the sight of their goal, gathered their forces for one magnificent spurt, and just as the mob reached the other end of the street, the ladies hurried up the gangplank.

The doctor, seeing them safely on board, refused to go with them. "I have ways of hiding until the mob disperses," he said, "and I must go back, for the others may need me in the hospital." He did not tell them of the sinister light he had seen hovering over the city. He said good-by to Little Small-Feet and with a lingering look at the sweet face and wistful eyes of the lady, he was gone.

As soon as possible they hurried to their cabin and before long Little Small-Feet was fast asleep, safe in the thought that she was leaving her old enemies behind forever. Her friend had been through too much that night to think of repose. The fate of the hospital was still in doubt and she followed in thought each step the doctor took on his return. Little Small-Feet did not awaken until the noonday sun struck full on her face; then turning she saw her friend sitting close beside her.

"Well, my child, you have had a long sleep and soon we must have tiffin. There are several foreigners on board and I think it is time you were known by some other name than Little Small-Feet. That is all right for a child but hardly dignified enough for a young lady who hopes some day to be a doctor. Shall I introduce you by the name of Dong Hsie Yin?[1] That is the name you were baptized by last year and a beautiful name it is, but, of course, when we are alone I shall always call you Little Small-Feet."

Thus for the third time the child received a name, but in her heart of hearts she always liked Little Small-Feet the best, and begged her dearest friends to call her that. To strangers she was known as Dong Hsie Yin.

When the river steamer at length drew up beside the bund, at the City by the Sea, Little Small-Feet exclaimed with pleasure at the strange buildings and all the noise and bustle.

"Ah," she laughed, "I am coming into a new world with a new name, and now I can forget all my old enemies." Little Small-Feet did not realize that old foes might cling as fast as the old name.

Hsie Yin passed three very eventful days in the City by the Sea, for each moment was filled with unusual sights. It was always a treat to pass down the broad streets with their overhanging balconies and bright signs covered with gilt characters, and going to the bund to watch the river thronged with every kind of native junk, and foreign craft never lost its charm. On the fourth day as they stood under the trees of the park, a ricksha drew up in front of them and their good friend, the doctor, stepped out. Little Small-Feet smiled a glad welcome and wondered why her guardian turned so white and then such a charming pink.

"It is really you!" the lady stammered. "I have not been able to rest for fear of what might have happened to you and the hospital."

"Well," he replied, "we had a pretty hot time for a few hours. Thank God, no one was hurt, but the hospital was burned and they are sending me home to raise money for another."

A very happy trio returned to the house that day; Little Small-Feet went on in front and the other two followed her slowly. The news about the hospital and a life work undone was indeed a sad blow to the Great Helpful Lady, but the thought that none of her friends had fallen victims to the mob compensated a little for the loss and relieved her mind of a dread that had haunted her ever since she had said good-by to the doctor on that awful night.

The two friends walked slower and slower, while Hsie Yin unconsciously quickened her pace to watch a funeral procession that, with great wailing of hired

---

[1] "Dong" is the family name; "Hsie Yin" means "Thankful for mercy."

mourners, was coming down the cross street. The gay gowns of the priests and the handsome trappings of the sedan chairs held her spellbound, and she never noticed a figure that came skulking up beside her until a birdlike claw was laid upon her arm. Then she turned in horror to see the leering features of Old Scarred Face almost touching her. With a scream of terror, Little Small-Feet snatched her arm away and turned to flee, never noticing in her horror which direction she took. Was the Goddess of Mercy watching over the girl at last or, rather, the guardian angels of her lady's psalm? Fortunately for her, she ran straight into the arms of her approaching friends. Had she made another turn, this story of Little Small-Feet would have ended right here or would never have been written.

"What is the matter? What in the world has happened?" her guardian exclaimed. With gasping breath the girl explained. The doctor hurried forward in pursuit but when he reached the corner there was no sign of the woman; she had completely disappeared.

"I thought I was safe forever," Little Small-Feet sobbed. "Do you suppose she will follow me to the end of the world?"

Her friends assured her that Old Scarred Face could not afford the price of the steamer fare, but they acknowledged to themselves that the woman must be in deadly earnest to have followed them so quickly and to have paid the necessary passage on the river boat.

From that time forward Hsie Yin was never permitted to be alone either in the house or on the street, and their cabins were engaged for the first steamer that sailed to America. On the day they went away the doctor, who was to remain behind for a month on business, came to the launch to see them off. While the two older people were engrossed in conversation, Little Small-Feet went to the rail to watch the crowd, for it was an absorbing sight to see strangers from every nation of the globe. Hsie Yin became so interested that she did not realize that it was time to start until she heard the doctor's voice in her ears speaking to her.

"Good-by, Little Small-Feet," he said; "take good care of your Great Helpful Lady, for she has promised to be my lady too." Then he turned and walked down the gangplank.

Little Small-Feet was so surprised that she could not think what he meant. Was her guardian going to desert her just as they had launched out on their great adventure? One glance at her friend's face reassured her, and being too interested in their departure to ask any questions, she turned to look at the wharf where the doctor was standing. The ropes were cast off from the dock and their launch began to fall slowly down the stream. The girl lifted her eyes a minute from the doctor to look at a pile of crates standing near him. Her astonished gaze fell upon the pock-marked features and dreaded scowl of Old Scarred Face, rendered even more malignant by thwarted spite. She fascinated Little Small-Feet as a snake does its prey and, try as she could, the girl could not turn her eyes away from her old enemy. The last human being, therefore, that Hsie Yin saw when she left her native land was the face of her most dreaded foe and, although she could not hear them, the curses of the woman seemed to ring in her ears.

It takes an old and experienced sailor to enjoy the cross currents of the Yellow Sea, and on the first day out Hsie Yin was sick; no one had ever been so ill before, she thought; she could not lift her head from the pillow, and she was absolutely certain that by the end of the three weeks there would be no Little Small-Feet left to tread the longed-for streets of the City by the Golden Gate. She even shed a tear or two of sympathy for her dear lady who, she knew, would grieve at her untimely end, and for her country to which she could never bring life and healing. She did not guess how many times travelers had imagined the same things before.

By the end of the second day, however, when the soft, gray haze slowly turned into the mountains and cliffs of old Japan, Hsie Yin had recovered sufficiently to be on deck and watch with a dawning interest the fast approaching shore. During the next few days the girl felt that at length she had sailed into fairyland, for all past troubles and dread of the future voyage were lost in the enjoyment of the moment. The blue of the sky, where whole fleets of white clouds sailed, wafted hither and thither by wayward breezes, was reflected in the clear water below. The tiny islands that dotted the sea were robed in every shade of green, from the light green of the terraced rice fields to the feathery bamboo and the darker shades of the pines, and beneath these quaint, gnarled pines the curved roof of a temple or the arch of a stone torii could be seen, or perhaps some wayside inn or farmer's cottage. The village streets and houses, which scrambled up the hillside and clung there in spite of all of the laws of gravitation, were also a wonder and delight to both travelers.

"I did not know that there were such lovely spots," Hsie Yin would exclaim; "I never thought that any country could be so beautiful as mine, and of course I never could love it in the same way, but I am sure that the king of the fairies must live here."

The sunsets and sunrises, too, turned all their loveliness to gold and pink and sapphire with lemon-yellow, mauves, and soft greens all blending into one, colors which no paint box ever held and which are the despair of artists. It was one long week of beauty and of ecstasy until the adjectives of the dictionary were exhausted and the senses were almost drunk with color. At the end they sailed at sunset up the famous Yokohoma Bay. Above it, rising like a cloud that the slightest breeze could waft away, was the cone of the sacred mountain, the dazzling white of the snow kissed to a delicate pink by the setting sun.

> "A snow-peak in the silver skies
> Beyond that magic world,
> We saw the great volcano rise
> With incense o'er it curled,
> Whose tiny thread of rose and blue
> Has risen since time began,
> Before the first enchanter knew
> The peak of old Japan."

It seemed almost a sacrilege to set foot on these fairy shores, but when they landed the friends were as delighted as they had been on the deck of the steamer. They reveled in the quaint, winding streets, the picturesque costumes of the people and, in the evening, the flickering of the lanterns carried by the ricksha coolies, looked like some giant fireflies dancing hither and thither.

The steamer waited a whole day in the harbor in order to take on cargo and the passengers were free to spend the time as they wished. Hsie Yin and her lady decided to take the train to see the famous Daibutsu that sits majestically in its park, apparently unconscious of the pilgrims that come from near and far to do it homage.

It was Little Small-Feet's first ride in a rail road train and though to her friend it seemed like a toy imitation of the real thing, to the girl it was a never-ceasing wonder. By this time, however, she had seen so many new and strange sights that she took it all more quietly and as a matter of course. The Daibutsu struck an answering chord in her breast. He seemed to symbolize the contemplative spirit of the Far East that she was to leave behind, perhaps for years.

"I like his calm and his quietness," she said, "I hope that I shall never get so hurried that I can not sit and think on the great matters of life."

"Yes, he is restful," her friend replied, "but he is too unmindful of the trouble and sorrow around him; I want a God whose face shows the lines of sorrow, who bears a mark of the scars."

"You are right; I had not thought of that; Daibutsu does not look as if he would care a bit if all the children were caught by Old Scarred Face."

All the way back Hsie Yin was quite subdued, for the mention of Old Scarred Face had cast a shadow over her. A whole week had passed and she had forgotten the woman's existence, but now she had an almost superstitious dread that her spell was still upon her.

At the station they again climbed into rickshas and were swiftly drawn toward the steamboat landing. Hsie Yin's coolie went so rapidly that he paid no attention to a ricksha coming down a side street and had to turn suddenly to avoid an accident. The two men drew up just long enough for Little Small-Feet to get a clear glance at the face of the passenger in the other vehicle. What was her horror to see the sallow features and sly smile of Creeping Sin! Then as she drew back in terror, his ricksha turned and disappeared into the gathering dusk.

Nothing more occurred to alarm them until they reached the wharf and boarded the launch; this was the last point of call before they left the Orient and its charms, its wonderful fascination, and its heartrending sorrows behind, and turned their faces toward the land of the to-morrow. If only they had been assured that they had left Creeping Sin behind as well they would have rested more easily. Why had he come to Japan?

How had he heard of their plans, or was this meeting a pure accident? There seemed to be no solution to the question.

The next morning Little Small-Feet awoke very early, and as she could not drop off to sleep again, she decided to go out on deck for a breath of air. She suddenly opened the door and stepped out into the corridor, nearly overturning their bedroom steward who had evidently been standing listening to their conversation. Very much startled, Hsie Yin returned to her friend and throwing herself on the couch burst into tears.

"What have I done?" she cried, "that I should be so tormented?"

"Well, my dear," her friend replied, "you have done nothing, but I am sure that when we have reached the other side we can throw them off. Surely they have more profitable things to do than to follow a child with no money and no connections. I have told you that the doctor has friends in the State Department, and if this persecution continues, we will have these people arrested and sent home. You know that when I promised to become the doctor's wife, he declared that he would look out for you as if you were his very own. I am glad that you will not be without the protection of a man, who will understand, much better than I, how to handle the matter."

"You will have to go back long before I am educated though, and then whatever will become of me?"

"We will never go until we are sure that you are safe. Then you will come and join us and it is my dream that the three of us can begin the work that we planned long ago."

Comforted by this thought, Hsie Yin dried her eyes and began to feel better. The stewardess at this moment entered with a cup of tea and the gossip of the steamer.

"Yes," she said, "there are many Chinese gentlemen traveling these days and a fine lot of trouble they make with all their servants and their meals that have to be cooked by their own chefs. There is a grand nobleman who has the best suite on this steamer. They say that his name is Lord Chang and he's some kin to the Emperor. I don't care who he is, he's a mean one if ever there was one. He's going to the exhibition to represent the Empress Dowager, and he is that mad about it, because he hates foreign countries, but she made him go. There's a friend of his traveling with him who has a sly smile; he gives a liberal tip, but I can't stomach his look at all; he's a bad one, he is, and up to no good! He sticks to his cabin and never goes out, but his servants are always underfoot."

The stewardess was mistaken in part of her in formation, for Creeping Sin and Lord Chang were not traveling in the same party, but Creeping Sin had chosen to sail on the steamer with the nobleman for his own purpose. Very recently the two bitter enemies had become partners in crime. How it happened no one knew except the wily Spider, and he for obvious reasons would not explain.

When the tiffin gong sounded and the rest of the passengers had hastened to the dining salon, Lord Chang and Creeping Sin had a meeting in the latter's suite. Creeping Sin received his guest with every courtesy and talked in an oily, unctuous tone very different from the coarse manner he was accustomed to use to Old Scarred Face.

"Yes," he said, "as always your honor speaks the truth. These foreigners will ruin our noble land and I for one would like to see every one of them dropped into the depths of the sea. But it must be handled with care. When you see their armies and navies as I have done in my journeys to their accursed countries, you will realize that it requires caution. It will take time but we can outwit them.

Do you know that on this very steamer there is a beautiful Chinese girl whom they have stolen? They are taking her to their own country, they say, to educate her. They will do this more and more until our land of blessed calm will be in a turmoil like their own, with no peace anywhere, our gods forgotten, and our beloved Confucius a byword and a contempt. Every child who receives their foreign education becomes a menace to the Empire. Soon the good old days of the sages will be gone forever."

Lord Chang ground his teeth at this news. "This must be stopped," he exclaimed. "You are clever at such things, cannot you manage to have her disappear? I might perhaps be able to arrange that no questions are asked. You concoct some story and I will indorse it. You must do it frequently in your business."

"It would be a delicate matter and would cost more than I care to put into it. The officials of the City by the Golden Gate have an undue prejudice against some of my activities. I will undertake the commission only under the condition that I may dispose of her as I please, but I can give little time to the affair for I have other game to follow."

"For five hundred dollars I will give you every right to her," replied Lord Chang.

"Why should I pay for the trouble I am to take and the risk I have to run?" asked the accomplice.

"You can sell her for five thousand taels if she is as beautiful as you say," returned Lord Chang. "Official protection has to be well paid for in matters of this kind; it is a great risk for me to wink at such matters and might endanger the Empire."

They bickered back and forth until Lord Chang compromised on half the sum. Few people knew that the nobleman had bartered his daughter for the paltry sum of two hundred and fifty dollars. In fact many long years were to pass before he realized it himself, but when he had left the cabin Creeping Sin sat and gloated with the old, sly smile on his face.

# Chapter VIII
# Little Small-Feet Takes a Journey

> And o'er us the whole of the soft blue sky
> Flashed like fire as the world went by,
> And far beneath us the sea like fire
> Flashed in one soft blue brilliant stream,
> And the journey was done, like a change in a dream.
>
> —Alfred Noyes.

Creeping Sin kept very closely to his own rooms. He was too busy over his schemes to care that the seas were blue and that flying fish with a flash of silver in their fins were making a mad race to keep up with the ship. He paid no attention to the breezes that wandered in and out of the porthole and fluttered the curtains and rustled the papers, but the little breezes watched him closely, for they realized that here was a man to whom the fresh air of heaven, the bright sunlight, and the open highway were repugnant, and they wished to find out what schemes he was planning against the good and innocent.

Like a great, black spider, Creeping Sin sat in his cabin weaving a web to catch his victims. He thought of his last night in the City by the Sea and how Old Scarred Face had brought him word that Little Small-Feet was to sail on this very steamer. With a wicked joy they had planned to make her own father deliver her into their hands. He had been careful to warn Old Scarred Face that she would reap no benefit from the capture; her only reward must be the knowledge that she had had her revenge on the child and her protectors. He had never seen her venom so plainly shown, and even he shuddered when he thought that some day that malice might be turned against himself.

"We have scorched the beehive and have driven the bees away forever," chuckled the woman. "After the burning of the hospital they will never dare return to the city."

"You will not see the girl again unless you visit the City by the Golden Gate, and the ocean is too deep and broad for you to walk across," grinned Creeping Sin, "but you can rest your heart in the thought that she shall pay double for all the trouble she has cost us." Old Scarred Face laughed harshly at his words although she would have much preferred dealing out her own vengeance.

Creeping Sin mused on all these things, and then began to scheme the kidnaping of Little Small-Feet. He laid his toils carefully and seemed to think of every contingency but he failed to take into consideration the fact that innocence and virtue can walk unscathed through plots and snares. He had never heard of Una and the Lion.

Hsie Yin's days were one long suspense and dread for she felt conscious that silken threads were being wound around her, threads that she could not break because they were invisible and placed by such cunning hands. The two friends were on the alert night and day and their imaginations frequently gave them false alarms so that they started at the slightest sound. Several times they ran into blue, skulking figures hidden in dark corners or heard furtive footsteps in their corridor at night, so that their fears were not groundless.

The beautiful harbor of the City of the Golden Gate was approached with much suspense. Would they be able to elude their pursuer here? The Great Helpful Lady mapped out her course of action. She expected to be met by friends who were very influential in the city and decided to appeal to them for assistance and, if necessary, for police protection; with such aid, she thought, they ought to be safe.

Fortunately their luggage was light and they could hurry through the customhouse, the only danger of delay being at the immigration office, and they had little fear of detention there as the doctor had been at great pains to see that Hsie Yin's entrance papers were properly signed and sealed.

Creeping Sin had already made up his mind what he would do. He had a shrewd knowledge of what a little clever tipping often accomplished, and his only fear was that his passport, which was forged, might be confiscated. He was conscious that his activities had often been frowned on by the better element in the city, but he felt confident that he could enter by means of bluff and bribes. He even suggested to Lord Chang that he would like to enter as a member of his retinue, but Lord Chang, not being able to see anything in it for himself, and having lost a large sum in fan-tan to Creeping Sin, said that it was not convenient and the matter was dropped. Creeping Sin, however, added this last item to the other grudges he had against Lord Chang to be settled at some future date. When he reached the underground world of Chinatown, he was confident that the kidnaping of Little Small-Feet would be an easy matter because he had often managed little affairs of this kind with the greatest ease.

On the day of the landing, however, the guardian angels did their very best for Hsie Yin, and Creeping Sin's attendant demons must have been away on a vacation for they did not help him in the least. The ladies' friends met them at the wharf, listened to their story with the greatest attention, and at once took up the matter.

"He is the very man we are looking for," exclaimed one of the gentlemen. "We have a reform government here at present which is trying to clean up Chinatown. If the man you speak of is the one I think he is, he owns one of the largest gambling places here. The police have been after him for months but he disappeared and evidently went back to his own country. They had a suspicion that he might arrive on this steamer and are waiting for him at this moment. If you will describe him, I will notify the immigration officers."

Hsie Yin told of Creeping Sin's masklike countenance and sly smile in a very trembling voice and when she had finished the party hurried off the wharf. The ladies did not remain long in the city, feeling that it was wiser to put as many miles as possible between them and their tormentor, but before they left they had the satisfaction of knowing that Creeping Sin was spending the night in a detention shed; that his passport was suspected so the chances were that he would be deported.

Creeping Sin, at the moment when their train drew out of the station, was grinding his teeth in impotent rage. He had no clue as to who had betrayed him, but by all the gods that he knew he swore to have vengeance on the "foreign devils" and never to draw a quiet breath until he had the girl and her guardians in his power. In ten days' time, however, he was again on a steamer sailing back to his own country.

The morning Hsie Yin had landed she had watched with interest the greetings that were extended to Lord Chang and his suite by various prominent men in the city. It made her happy to feel that one of her countrymen should be treated with such honor, and she drew quite near to watch the ceremonies, but Hsie Yin did not suspect for a moment that it was her father that was being so feted. She was familiar enough with the faces of her enemies but her father and mother were strangers to her.

The ladies hurried at once to the Great Helpful Lady's family, who lived in a prosperous New England town where fine schools and educational opportunities abounded, and Hsie Yin plunged immediately into a new world. The months of adjustment were naturally very hard, because children from the Orient are a curiosity and are often treated as such by tactless strangers, but on the whole Hsie Yin was received cordially and after the first few months she felt herself quite at home. One fact added greatly to her comfort: she found that in this particular city she was the only person from her own land, and she felt that here at least there could be no danger from Old Scarred Face.

After a year her Great Helpful Lady and the doctor were married and again returned to their work, leaving Little Small-Feet in the hands of friends who promised to give her a home and watch her progress with the most painstaking care. This home was plain but full of the best kind of culture and refinement; there were no luxuries but every necessity. In work and play the years went rapidly by until Little Small-Feet at length entered college, and the first milestone on the road to her ambition was reached.

At the university Hsie Yin was a great favorite, for her scholarship, her sense of humor, and her quiet dignity made her both popular and respected. She absorbed and naturally enjoyed what was best in literature, art, and music, and perhaps it was her ancestry that made her appreciate the luxurious houses of some of her friends, for in them there was more that was akin to her early home than in the plainer New England town where she had attended school. Little Small-Feet never lost sight of her goal, however, and often as she lay on her soft bed, her thoughts would wing back to the beggar children of her land who were roaming the winter streets clad in rags, and she would vow to herself never to allow the love of luxury to keep her from devoting her life to the outcasts.

The years flew by, happy and full of interest, and with no room in them for thoughts of Creeping Sin and Old Scarred Face. Why should she worry over them when they were thousands of miles away? She felt positive that they had forgotten her existence, because her lady's letters never mentioned them, but were always full of plans for the future.

Two years of college life passed like a breath and then Hsie Yin entered the medical school. Her shapely fingers seemed formed for no other purpose than to perform skillful operations, and her quick brain caught a thing in a flash, so that she was the joy of her professors and secretly the envy of many of the students. Surely at last the spell wrought upon her by the spirits of the pagoda had passed away! Was it their magic that had changed an Oriental princess into a modern woman wrapped up in her profession? Unfortunately Wang Dah Mah, the authority on such matters, was not there to say.

Once through her medical course, Hsie Yin decided to take a special course in eye work and children's diseases, deferring her return to her own land for another year, and during this time an event occurred that upset her nerves and shook her resolution to return to work in the Flowery Kingdom.

## Little Small-Feet Takes a Journey

It happened one snowy day, when the winter winds were blowing shrilly down the street, that Hsie Yin came out from her clinic and stood waiting for a street car. The whirling snow had partly covered the tracks and delayed traffic, so that she wondered if the cars were running, and finally decided to try to walk. The girl's road lay past a Chinese laundry where she had frequently left her collars and cuffs, because she liked to encourage her hard-working countrymen. As Little Small-Feet opened the door of the shop, the noise of the storm drowned the sound of her entrance and she could see two men talking in an inner room, although they did not observe her.

One of the men was clearly her friend, the laundryman, and he was listening to his companion with great respect and even a little fear. The second man was a great contrast to his companion; he was clad in rich satin; every hair of his long, silky queue was in order and tied with a handsome tassel; and his thin, tapering fingers wore their nails two inches long. Little Small-Feet was about to call for her bundle when the stranger turned and she found herself looking into the false face and sly, triumphant smile of Creeping Sin.

"I told you I knew that it was she," he exclaimed, in a southern dialect, and started for ward to seize the startled girl.

It was fortunate for Little Small-Feet that her doctor's training had taught her to be on the alert. She darted quickly forward and out into the now blinding storm, whose wicked wind seemed to jeer at her terror as it came rushing down the street. Blinded by the storm and not able to hear the swift footstep of her pursuer, she struggled on. As she came to the corner a car in front of her stopped to let off a passenger, and she, not waiting to see which way it went, hurried on board.

It was a very sad and disheartened Hsie Yin that dragged her way into her rooms that night. After all these years her enemies were still on her track, and if she returned to her own land how could she hope to be safe? All night long the winds howled around the house, seeming to mock at her and her ambitions and assuring her that she could never hope to carry them out against adversaries such as these.

Early the next day Hsie Yin consulted her friends as to what course she ought to pursue and the professors in the university took up the case. The laundryman was arrested and questioned, but all that he could say was:

"Me not know verry muchee; he heepee bad man. Chinese all hatee. Owes Sam Lee monee. Gone now."

Which was not reassuring at all, but the police promised to be on the watch and to arrest anyone answering to the description of Creeping Sin. But what could be done to him, should he be arrested, was not very clear, unless he could be deported.

There were many things that were still less clear to Hsie Yin. How had Creeping Sin found out where she was and what was he planning to do? The police seemed to think that he must be the head of one of the Chinese secret societies which are very mysterious and to which many of the Chinese in this country belong. But who could tell?

All the ease and comfort of the past few years dropped like a mantle from Little Small-Feet's shoulders and her future looked very doubtful. Finally she thought of her lady's guardian angels and her friend's calmness through the riot, and her fears began to subside. There was a force that was even greater than Creeping Sin's and she must prove it.

The whole of the following July Hsie Yin spent in the baby hospital. The heat seemed like a heavy blanket but she worked bravely on, up held by the thought of a vacation in August. A month was to be spent at the seaside with one of her college classmates, in a home where every luxury would be provided. As she went down the long wards, the thought of the waves splashing on the shore seemed to give her strength. And then at length the happy day arrived and she started gayly off in the hope of a holiday free from care.

The place was all that she had dreamed and nature and friends seemed to conspire to make everything delightful. There were gardens and lawns around the house, gardens that were the envy of the countryside. Larkspur and phlox and every shade of yellow made great splashes of color against gray stone walls, and beyond the great blue Atlantic rolled. Was it any wonder, then, that the back of Hsie Yin's dreams were haunted by dim memories of an other garden where lotus and goldfish ponds abounded, a garden full of stone lanterns and little winding paths, where poppies danced full to hot summer breezes as they did here? In vain did the girl's waking thoughts try to visualize and name this dream garden, but she decided that it was only the result of her sleeping imaginations.

As the month slowly passed she felt as if the luxury of the palace were sapping her desire for work. Each day it seemed harder to think of going back to the life of hardship she had marked out for helself. How pleasant it would be always to live such a care-free existence, away from the shadow of Old Scarred Face and Creeping Sin. At first Hsie Yin brushed these fancies hastily aside, but as time went on they persisted and followed her relentlessly.

One day, after a morning spent in idleness over the latest novel, a letter was handed to Little Small-Feet. When she had read the first few lines, she almost let it fall in amazement, for it contained an offer that would make it possible for her to remain in this country, away from the menace of her old enemies. The offer was truly amazing in the light of her nationality and antecedents, for one of the leading women's medical schools was inviting her to become a member of their faculty, with the most flattering allusions to her work in the past and a truly tempting salary. The only person to whom Little Small-Feet showed this letter was her college classmate.

"Of course, you will accept an invitation like that; it would be suicidal to throw it aside!" the friend exclaimed.

"But think of all my plans and ambitions; my Great Helpful Lady did not educate me for such a position but to help my own countrywomen."

"Stuff and nonsense," answered her friend; "this is a practical age and we must meet it in a practical way. Talents such as yours would be thrown away in picking up beggar brats and caring for them."

"If my lady had felt that way, I should not be here," replied Hsie Yin.

Her friend was silenced a minute but she proceeded to the attack: "You have often told me that you want to pay back all your friends have spent on your education, and that some of them are not well off and need the money. If you accept this offer you can do it quickly, while the other way they may have to wait for years."

"Yes, but I have a feeling that they would rather never see a cent of it than that I should forget my own people."

These arguments nevertheless had great weight with Hsie Yin, and although she tried to make up her mind that there was no choice and that she must go back, the masklike face of Creeping Sin would come before her eyes and her resolution would weaken.

The August heat seemed to enervate her still further and Little Small-Feet felt all her desire for achievement gone. She longed for her lady, although in her heart of hearts she knew that in a case of this kind her friend would not interfere; the decision would be left to her own conscience.

"You are a dreamer and so is your lady. How much better to stay where you can live a long life doing good than be killed in the first year if you go back. You surely will be, you know. Besides there is plenty to be done in this country," her classmate would urge.

"Suppose you take the course and do it," answered Hsie Yin, "and I will go back to my country and they will never miss me here."

"I told you that you are a dreamer," her friend replied. "Just think what my parents would say if I became a doctor. How foolish it would be to stop in the middle of my course in interior decoration and take up medicine! Why, my family would all think me insane!"

When the girl had left the room, Hsie Yin thought to herself: "Alice and I do not speak the same language, that is very evident. I really ought to leave before I accept all her standards." But the life of ease was too pleasant for her to care to change and as she had no excuse for not finishing her visit, Hsie Yin drifted along from day to day.

One evening her friends invited Little Small-Feet to go on a moonlight sail. It was a wonderful night, with just the right kind of breeze, and the rippling waves laughed along the shore. The next morning the answer to the invitation from the medical school must be sent, so Hsie Yin resolutely refused the sail, determined that the hour had arrived when she must make her decision.

After the party had left for the boat, Hsie Yin strolled down to the beach and seated herself on the sands. The sea and headlands were bathed in moonlight, and it would be hard to surpass the soft beauty of the scene. But Hsie Yin felt on this night that she had no part in all the beauty; it hurt though it allured her. In her agony of soul, she drove her hands down into the sands beaten hard by the surf, unconscious of what she was doing, for her thoughts were thousands of miles away, following the footsteps of a beggar child who was toiling over mountain passes or begging in dirty city streets, and beside the girl, haunting her footsteps, she could see the gaunt form of a beggar woman.

Surely no one could ask her to face such hardships, such dangers, as her future life would entail if she returned to her own people. Hsie Yin thought of the physical discomforts, the poverty, the dirt, and the disease, and above all she heard the cries of the mob as they had sounded on the night when she and her friend had fled through the darkness. Little Small-Feet's family, too, had deserted her; her foes had hounded her from the land. She owed her country and her people nothing. Her thoughts told her that she had the opportunity of becoming truly famous if she should accept this position. There was a chance to blaze a trail; already she had made suggestions in the treatment of children's diseases that had proved of great benefit. Why stop all this work to undertake the perilous task that she had set out to do? So ran her thoughts this moonlit evening.

Then stealing over the water came the sound of singing from one of the boats:

> "By the old Moulmein Pagoda, lookin' eastward to the sea,
> There's a Burma girl a-settin', and I know she thinks o' me;
> For the wind is in the palm-trees, and the temple-bells they say:
> 'Come you back, you British soldier; come you back to Mandalay!'

> "Come you back to Mandalay,
>   Where the old Flotilla lay;
>   Can't you 'ear their paddles chunkin' from Rangoon to Mandalay?
>   On the road to Mandalay,
>   Where the flyin'-fishes play,
>   An' the dawn comes up like thunder outer China 'crost the Bay!"

Hsie Yin listened, half-heeding, then more attentively. There was something to be said in the favor of the Far East after all, and it was a Western poet who said it. Strange, indeed, that he should interpret its spirit to this child of the Orient. As the music went on she listened still more closely, and a big longing surged up within her to see the mists on the rice fields again, and the groves of feathery bamboo, and to hear the song of the coolies as they swing along under their heavy burdens. As she half caught the words of the song, her thoughts flew to the summer she had spent with her lady in the mountains, and a conversation which they had had there one evening just at sunset.

"Are there not many doctors and nurses in your so great and noble country?" she remembered asking her teacher.

"Yes, Little Small-Feet, many, many hundred," her friend had replied.

"Well, if they studied to be nurses and doctors for the sake of helping people, I should think they would go where they were needed the most; I know I would," she had responded, and she recollected how carefully the lady had explained to her that the reason that they did not go was because they did not know the need.

These thoughts, with many others, came surging in upon Hsie Yin and made her feel as if her own words would condemn her, for if any one knew the needs, she did and here she was faltering in her resolution. By this time the song was nearly over and Little Small-Feet again began to listen:

> "But that's all shove be'ind me—long ago an' fur away,
>   An' there ain't no 'busses runnin' from the Bank to Mandalay;
>   An' I'm learnin' 'ere in London what the ten-year soldier tells:
>   'If you've 'eard the East a-callin', you won't never 'eed naught else.'
>     No! you won't 'eed nothin' else
>     But them spicy garlic smells,
>     An' the sunshine an' the palm-trees an' the tinkly temple-bells."

Yes, Hsie Yin heard the East acalling her, but it was with a different voice than that of which the British sang; it was the cry of pain and anguish, the wail of helpless children and the moans of hopeless womanhood. How had she been deaf to it for a single moment! What had deadened her sympathy so that she could not see her duty?

Little Small-Feet's struggle was not quite over, however. She thought of Old Scarred Face and Creeping Sin, of the painful death she might be called upon to suffer, and again her courage wavered. But once more memory of her lady came to her, and the day when they had hidden on the wharf. She recalled how she had said to her friend, "And are you suffering all this for me?" and her lady had replied, "There was One that suffered more than this for me, Little Small-Feet."

Then at length Hsie Yin came to her decision. When she thought of Gethsemane and the way of the cross, there could be no shrinking. She must respond to the call of the East.

That night Hsie Yin slept peacefully and in her dreams she seemed to hear pagoda bells softly swinging back and forth, touched into sweet music by the wayward breezes.

The next morning there came a letter from Little Small-Feet's own country telling her that the doctor and her old friend were earnestly longing and expecting her return. Part of the letter ran thus:

"You will be happy to learn that the three of us have been appointed to carry on the work at 'The City of the Blue Pagoda.' You have probably never heard of the place, but it is an important town two weeks' journey into the interior. It is rather anti-foreign, so your help will be invaluable to us in opening up the work. A little start has already been made in a dispensary, and the funds are on hand for a men's and a women's hospital. We want you to bring all the latest wrinkles in hospital buildings and other things. We are glad that we are to be sent so far away from any place that you have ever seen, and that there will be no chance there of meeting Old Scarred Face and Creeping Sin who seem to have completely disappeared. We suggest, however, that you keep as quiet as possible in the City by the Sea and sail directly for the City of the Blue Pagoda without visiting the City Lying in the Shadow of Purple Mountain, as we know you long to do. It is well to avoid publicity, so we have kept these plans to ourselves."

In a few days Little Small-Feet cabled the word, "Coming," to her distant friends, and with all her misgivings forgotten, she completed her preparations for her life work.

# Chapter IX
# The City of the Blue Pagoda

> Low and long forevermore
>     Where the Wonder-Wander Sea
> Whispers to the wistful shore
>     Purple songs of mystery,
> Down the shadowy quay we came
>     Though it hides behind the hill
> You will end it just the same
>     And the seamen singing still.
>
>         —Alfred Noyes.

There was much excitement in the City of the Blue Pagoda one clear November day. It is amazing how fast rumor flies in a country where there are few railroads and very little telegraphic communication; it almost seems miraculous the way gossip spreads over hill and dale into the out-of-the-way corners of the Flowery Kingdom. It was small wonder that many shook their wise heads and said that the spirits of the air were very busy this autumn, and some even went so far as to burn an extra incense stick or two before the household god although to many this seemed like a wild extravagance.

"Wait until the foreigners really come," they exclaimed. "It is foolish waste to spend money so freely on rumors brought by boat people."

"They swear by all they know that the strangers tried to talk price with them when they were at a port on the great river. But they refused to betray their native city by bringing barbarians to live within its walls. The sum they spoke of was large, too; it is not often that we find our boat people so worthy."

"Mark my words, there is something behind it; I never knew Lao Weh to refuse an offer where he could make a profit. There are doubts in my mind whether they talked with him at all."

"Well," replied the first woman, "it is an ill wind that is blowing over the city to-day. Here is Lord Chang returned after many years spent away and in an evil temper. Those who owe him money need to beware. And now the red-haired barbarians are coming also. It looks black in deed; it will be a cruel winter for the poor. Although they do say that foreigners have some wonderful magic by which they heal the sick. That man who had the dispensary opened last year cured old Song Sao Tze, who lives down by the south gate, of chills. He gave her little white pellets that were very bitter, but she has been well ever since. Lord Chang hates the foreigners and they will not rest here long if he can turn them out. He has to walk carefully, however, for ever since the Boxer revolution, the Government rather frowns on killing foreigners. They say that the Empress had to pay a million taels for every outlander killed."

"Lord Chang would think twice before stirring up trouble like that," cackled the second woman. "They say that every cash he is forced to spend takes a day off his life. He would fall dead if he should be called on for a million taels, although he could easily pay it."

"Old Wang Dah Mah told me he had to pay an enormous ransom for his part in the Boxer uprising, and that since then he hates the 'foreign devils' more than ever. Here she comes now; perhaps she can tell us whether there is any truth in these rumors."

Slowly down the street came Wang Dah Mah, looking very little older than when she used to crone lullabies over Little Small-Feet. The years have passed over her kindly, leaving only a few more wrinkles to mark the coming of age.

After a few polite questions, the woman fell into earnest conversation over the strange news they had received that day.

"I tell Lady Chang," commented Wang Dah Mah, "that the pagoda bells should be rung; it would be well worth the cash, if we have to pay it out of our own pockets. They were not ringing when Little Small-Feet was born and ill luck has followed the family ever since. True they have had a son and he is a fine child, and the crooked ways of Lord Chang he will not follow, but declares that he will go to foreign lands to be educated, instead of wisely studying the classics as all his ancestors have done. He has been truly bewitched, and he and Lord Chang are always quarreling; there is no peace between them. The foreigners at the capital have turned the child's head; they know so many evil enchantments. Lord Chang will have a fit of passion if he hears the rumor that the outlanders are coming to this city; he brought us all here to get young Lord Chang away from their influence."

"Well, Wang Dah Mah, you speak wisely," replied the woman. "The pagoda bells must surely be rung for the sake of ourselves and our children. But it would take a fortune to keep them ringing night and day. We must ask the priest if it will be sufficient to ring them the first day the foreigners arrive. Have you seen these barbarians yourself, and is it true that they have a hole bored in their chest, so that they may be carried from place to place by means of a pole thrust through their body?"

"I do not know," replied Wang Dah Mah. "For myself, I always keep at a safe distance and smell camphor to keep from being bewitched, but young Lord Chang says that it is stuff and nonsense and that they are made exactly like civilized people. He wanted to have a foreign woman doctor for his mother's cough, but of course we could not hear of it."

"The world is changing indeed when young men will not listen to their elders and are crazy for new things," answered the first woman.

"Yes, the Empress herself," replied Wang Dah Mah, "seems to have had her head turned and is having her portrait painted by a foreign woman artist."

"Fortunate it is for us, then, that the capital lies so many leagues away. The City of the Blue Pagoda has always been noted for its hatred of new things. The golden age lies in the past and what are we to try to improve on it? We must make it too hot for these barbarians; there are ways of doing it so that the officials can never trace the plotters."

"Well, for my part," commented the second woman, "it makes me feel more kindly toward the strangers when I hear that Lord Chang hates them so fiercely, for he always hates the good and loves the evil."

"There is nothing good in the 'foreign devils,' I can assure you of that," said Wang Dah Mah. "I know what I know and have seen what I have seen." This very vague condemnation impressed her friends mightily, for Wang Dah Mah was the only one of the three who had ever been outside the walls of the city. All that she knew of the foreigners had been gathered from the gossip of various yamens; she had never even spoken to one, and her prejudice was all the deeper for that reason.

When she returned to the home of Lord Chang, she carefully told her mistress all the news she had heard and they together agreed that the future looked dark.

"If these foreigners could cure this cough," sighed the lady, "I would almost risk their magic; my son urges me to try."

"Oh, my lady, do hot speak such words of ill omen! It is enough to bring the evil eye upon the household. The medicine our ancestors used is surely good enough for us."

"My son says that the old necromancer is a fool and that I shall die before he cures me."

"The old necromancer is a magician and knows exactly what you say at this minute, so do be careful, my lady, or it will cost many taels and perhaps your very existence."

"If only," sighed Lady Chang, "I could get one glimpse of Little Small-Feet, I would not care what became of me."

"It is also unwise to speak of her—remember what the priest in the temple said—although, I admit, I very often long for her myself. We are two wicked women," and Wang Dah Mah wiped her sleeve across her eyes.

Lady Chang and Wang Dah Mah held this discussion in the summer house overlooking the river. They were so deeply interested that they paid no attention to a houseboat which was at that moment turning the bend of the stream. A strong wind filled the tawny sails and made the ship fairly dance on the waves. Upon the deck stood Hsie Yin and her friends, eager for the first glimpse of their new home.

Nature had given a royal setting to the city, surrounded as it was with high mountains and clothed in bamboo groves and terraced paddy fields. As for the town with its high walls, tiled roofs, and quaint temples that adorned each knoll, and with its pagoda pointing like a tapering finger skyward, no description could portray its Oriental charm.

"To think that I ever hesitated about coming back," Hsie Yin sighed. "I must have been bewitched; the lure of the East would have haunted me all my days. Just compare the Flatiron Building to that," she continued, pointing to the soft colors of the blue pagoda. "Somehow I have a feeling that I have seen all this before; I can dimly remember climbing up into a balcony like one of those and being chased away by a black dog. I suppose it was in some other city, though, for when I was with Old Scarred Face, we visited hundreds, it seemed to me. They are all so dim and far away in my mind because I have tried my best to forget that time."

"How the little bells are blowing back and forth in this wind; they seem almost alive and ringing with a purpose!" exclaimed the lady.

On the other side of the boat stood the doctor and his native assistant, a fine, tall man with cultivated face and manner and the bearing of a gentleman. He turned at that moment and caught the lady's last remark.

"That is a good omen for our arrival," he remarked. "It may make all the difference between whether we are allowed to stay or are driven out. The people have a superstition that when the pagoda bells are ringing no evil can come to the city, but if any new event happens when the bells are quiet, the demons are busy and harm will befall. The people of this city, I am sorry to say, are very antiforeign and I had great difficulty in renting any house. The great Lord Chang lives here and he hates the strangers. As he has mortgages on a great deal of the property, no one in his power dares to lease land with out his consent. However, I managed to rent premises in a high part of the town, where we shall not be in danger from the floods. See, it is over there!" and he pointed to some buildings about half a mile from Lord Chang's residence. "It has been used for a small dispensary and hospital before and is well suited for our purpose until we can build."

At the name of Lord Chang, the two ladies looked at each other aghast. Surely he was the man who had crossed on the steamer with them and who was intimate with Creeping Sin; and they remembered that four years before he had become famous all over the world for his part in the Boxer movement! Had they run their heads into a hornet's nest? They comforted themselves with the fact that Lord Chang had refused to interfere to save Creeping Sin from deportation at the time of their voyage to America, and also that the nobleman had lost so much "face" in the Boxer troubles that he was scarcely likely to interfere again with foreigners.

"We're here and we cannot turn back," said the Great Helpful Lady, "so we must see it through. I am glad that we have you to counsel us, Pastor Meng. We have never forgotten how you hid us that day on the hulk when Old Scarred Face led the riot." Pastor Meng had been trained as an evangelist because he had shown such stanch loyalty to the cause on the occasion of the first mob.

The anchor was finally lowered and a board was laid as a gangplank from the deck to the shore. A servant was sent to the city to bring chairs for the ladies, while the men busied themselves in collecting coolies to carry the luggage. Magic really must exist in the Far East, for at the slightest excitement men seem fairly to rise out of the ground. Hardly had the boat neared the shore, when one or two ragged boys appeared, apparently bent on staring the strangers out of countenance. Then a dog and a pig ambled into view and an old hag, who had come down to the river to do a bit of washing.

As soon as she saw the passengers, she put her hands to her mouth and screamed to a crony in a near-by hovel, "Hurry up, the foreign devils have come! and I cannot tell if they are men or women."

Two or three wheelbarrow men ran forward almost immediately, leaving the loads which they were taking to market and pressing down close to the edge of the river. By the time the chairs had arrived and the strangers could disembark, a really formidable crowd had collected and was in creasing every moment; the news, too, was spreading through the city like wildfire and they felt that the sooner they could get to cover the better. The people were not hostile, only vaguely curious, but they were far from complimentary in their comments.

One thing puzzled the rabble very much: in spite of all the rumors and gossip that had reached them, no word had been said of a Chinese lady being of the party, so when they saw Hsie Yin, they were quite mystified as to her identity. The fact that a cultured woman of their own race was with the foreigners made a good impression and kept the throng from an unfriendly act. It never entered their minds that Hsie Yin was a woman doctor, although they readily picked out the foreign gentleman as a physician.

"See, he carries a black bag," they whispered. "Probably in it are the bones of infants he will grind into powder."

The talking, yelling, and screaming continued for some time until at length the coolies were satisfied with the price offered to them and consented to take up their burdens and start for the city. It was an imposing throng and, as it proceeded, the procession grew longer and longer. Pastor Meng took them through the least frequented streets, but they were well weary of the crowd by the time they reached the wall that surrounded their own compound. The gate was thrown open with a magnificent gesture by their ragged gatekeeper, and with a sigh of relief, they heard it swing to behind them.

At length they had shut out the world with its curious eyes and unkind comments, although the long night through they could hear the voices of the loafers, and knew that many people were coming and going, ready at the slightest spark to flame into mischief. Until early morning the beating of drums could be heard and the flare of bonfires seen, and their servants assured them that pious souls in the city had paid a large sum to the priests to propitiate the evil spirits, who might be angered at the approach of barbarians into their domain. The stranger never forgets the first night he spends in a heathen city, with the weird cries and barking dogs and the life of the city pulsing around him.

The new quarters were low native houses built around picturesque courts. The quadrangle of their home separated the men's and women's buildings. These wards opened each on their own courts and had separate entrances from the street, so that patients need not invade the seclusion of the family. Each tiny hospital had a dispensary and guest room and was absolutely independent of the other.

"I have engaged a room for a chapel about a li away," explained Pastor Meng, "where I will preach and have services. It seemed better in case of a riot not to have the hospital too near. My wife and family are already settled on an other street."

Pastor Meng, like the good fairy he was, had thought of many devices to make them comfortable. He had had wooden floors laid over the earthen pavement, and glass put in all the windows, and some beautiful native furniture, that could be bought for a song, installed in the dining room. The rest he had left to the ladies to settle. There were some things, however, that even the skilled hands of Pastor Meng could not do; he could not keep the rats from running over the ceiling made of bamboo mats, nor the scorpions from dropping from the same mats directly on the dining-room table. Such incidents are taken as a matter of course in the Middle Kingdom.

The ladies at once went to work to settle the house and the hospital, but they were very much hampered in this undertaking by a constant stream of curious visitors. To avoid the suspicion of dark deeds, everything must of course be open for inspection; one day's reception was not enough, it must go on day and night, week in and week out, until all were satisfied. Oh, the weariness of spirit that comes from answering the same question over and over when one wants to be putting away stores or tidying up kitchens! And, oh, the vast amount of tea that was consumed—enough, the Great Helpful Lady declared, to float an ocean steamer! The only thought that upheld them was the knowledge that allaying suspicion was as necessary a part of their work as dressing wounds or nursing typhoid patients.

Until after the Christmas they had no patients whatsoever; distrust was too deeply ingrained for that. In fact, only the very poorest and lowest of the women would come to them as servants. These women, having no reputation to lose, did not care what the neighbors said, but the efficient, decent amahs kept away from them altogether.

When the discouragement of it all pressed upon them too heavily, they would take chairs and go for rides outside the city gates. When they were far away from the curious crowds on the mountain side, they would leave their chairs and wander up and down the winding paths through the groves of bamboo, and rest their spirits by drinking in the many varied and enchanting views. They discovered the Temple of the Dragon Pool, and the priests, an idle set, but with hospitable instincts, would offer them tea and allow them to sit by the hour under the shade of the willows, and their walks had to be finally curtailed because a wild rumor reached them that people were saying that the foreigners were hunting for gold and hidden treasure, and held converse with evil spirits in these walks, in the hopes that the demons would show them secret stores.

Hsie Yin's first case was the old woman from the south gate, who had been cured of malaria by the former doctor. She was so poor and miserable that she scarcely cared if they did cast the evil eye upon her.

She had cut her hand and it was in bad condition and covered with dirt and rags. When Hsie Yin began to dress it, the woman started back in surprise.

"Not you, Miss Hsie Yin, not you! Why you are a lady; let the foreigner do it. It was never heard that a Chinese lady should be a doctor; that is not our custom."

Hsie Yin explained to her that nevertheless she had learned to be a doctor because her own countrywomen needed good care so much.

"Is it not more fitting that Chinese women should take care of their own sisters than to leave it all to the benevolent people of other countries?" she asked.

"There is some truth in that," replied the woman; "but are you sure that they have not bewitched you and is there no magic in your medicine?"

"None whatever, I swear to you!" replied Hsie Yin. "Would I, a loyal Chinese woman, try to bewitch my own people? The only magic we use is that of love and kindness."

"That is good magic and better than to acquire merit," answered the woman. "Your touch, gracious lady, is as light as the thistledown. The old quack doctor on our street wanted to burn me with red-hot needles, but I like your way best."

The hand began to heal quickly and the woman, who, though poor, had a wide circle of acquaintances, sang Hsie Yin's praises far and wide. It was some time, however, before anyone else was bold enough to come, and the winter was nearly gone before Hsie Yin had any patients who dared to trust themselves in the ward or would consent to an operation.

Had Hsie Yin's college classmate known of these discouragements, she would have nodded her head wisely and said: "I told you so. It would have been much better to have stayed where you were wanted, than to go where they do not appreciate you. I call it a winter wasted."

Hsie Yin, however, did not waste time. She spent these months of inactivity studying the Chinese classics, language, and etiquette, so that she might be better able to understand the heart of the people.

The first in-patient was a poor woman blind from a cataract, and a comparatively simple operation brought back her sight. When the bandages were removed and she saw the shape of things in the room and Hsie Yin's bright face, her joy knew no bounds.

"Why, Dr. Hsie Yin, you are a lady! I knew you had a sweet voice and a light touch but I never dreamed you were a lady! Why, you have waited on me like a servant!" she exclaimed.

"I wanted to make you well," replied Hsie Yin, "and I did it because I loved you, Li Sao Tze."

Li Sao Tze was forced to believe her because the love shone in every line of Hsie Yin's face.

"I don't understand it," murmured Li Sao Tze; "we Chinese talk of duty and filial piety but we do not talk about love, and we do not take strangers in and treat them as if they were our own blood. I never knew there could be places like this hospital. Do not send me away, honorable lady; let me always stay near you!"

It nearly broke Hsie Yin's heart to have to say "No" to the old woman, but the hospital was far too small to hold all grateful patients. She promised the good soul that she could see her frequently and occasionally she could do light cleaning at the hospital.

Hsie Yin's reputation grew and spread from the moment that Li Sao Tze returned to her home. Her neighbors came crowding in to hear of this amazing cure. It was soon abroad through the city that a Chinese lady had become a doctor and that she could make the blind see. The story grew and grew until it was commonly reported that both doctors could not only make the blind see, but that they could do it in cases where the eyes were gone from the sockets.

Li Sao Tze would talk to her old friend from the south gate, and the women of the neighborhood would listen open-mouthed to the marvels they would tell.

"Of course, the foreigners are quite mad," they would say. "None but crazy people would study to be doctors and ask so small a price, but it was a glad day for the poor when they came to this city. Did Lord Chang ever think of us or raise a finger for us? No! Give us these mad foreigners every time!"

The crowd would nod the approval they felt, but sometimes one or two would say,

"Such talk is not safe; if Lord Chang hears, he will run you all out of the city."

Hsie Yin's practice grew apace. Some came from real ailments and many more from curiosity, but in some way, by the charm of her manner and her ready sympathy, she won them all and "those who came to scoff remained to pray." When the hot summer months came on, the friends consulted as to whether they should not rent part of the Temple by the Dragon Pool for a month and get a little rest and change. The air was very sultry in their compound and the attendance at the hospitals not quite so large, so when August finally arrived, with its dog days and its sickening odors, they decided to retreat to the mountain side, glad of such a refuge.

One or two weeks slipped by in idleness or in exploring some of the out-of-the-way mountain paths. This had to be done with discretion as villagers assured them that two tigers had recently been seen in this vicinity. The doctor always carried a revolver and took the lead in these excursions, but nothing wilder than a sheep was encountered.

Twice a week the doctor went down to the city for a clinic and to keep in touch with the situation there. One day at the beginning of the third week of their stay, he went down, but at evening he did not return as usual. They waited until late in the evening, consumed with anxiety. Had he met the tiger? Was there a riot in the city? The temple was not a safe place for two women to remain alone. What should they do?

Just as they were about to give him up for the night, their trusted servant appeared with coolies and two chairs. He handed them a note from the doctor which read:

"Cholera has broken out in the city and I cannot leave. Neither is it safe for you to be alone in the temple overnight. I have sent the chairs so that you can return immediately, for we shall need every hand if we are to fight this plague. I have received a pass from the head official, so that the city gates will be left open and you can enter without trouble. Come as soon as possible!"

Cholera in the city! They would rather have met the tiger!

# Chapter X
# The Deadly Pestilence

> The black-barred moon was large and low
> When we came to the Forest of Ancient Woe;
>    And over our head the stars were bright.
> But through the forest the path was traveled
> Its phosphorescent aisle unraveled
>    In one thin ribbon of dwindling light:
> And twice and thrice on the fainting track
> We paused to listen. The moon grew black,
>    But the coolies' faces glimmered white,
> As the wild wood echoed in dreadful chorus
> A laugh that comes horribly hopping o'er us
>    Like monstrous frogs thro' the murky night.
>
> —Alfred Noyes.

One would scarcely choose a tiger-infested path in the heart of an unfriendly country for a quiet evening ramble, but under the circumstances Hsie Yin and her lady could not hesitate, for their duty lay in the city. They gathered their few possessions together in great haste, said good-by to the priests, and in the course of an hour were on the road.

The coolies were not at all in favor of this ad venture and the doctor had been forced to give them twice their regular pay before they would consent to leave the town. They very wisely considered tiger- and demon-haunted hills a poor place to be found after dark. The party had proceeded about one li when the men put down the chairs and refused to proceed unless more money was paid to them. The ladies pleaded in vain; the fellows would listen to no arguments and, to prove their determination, one man started down the path and disappeared into the shadows. Those left behind called and hallooed in vain, and in order to keep the other bearers, the friends were forced to yield. Lao Pong, the foreigners' faithful boy, took up the pole that the truant had dropped and again they moved forward.

For the first few li a new moon threw a feeble light along the path, but later the mists that arose from the ponds and lakes hid it completely and the bearers had to feel their way along. The mountain side was interlaced with many winding trails and in the darkness there was grave danger that the party would lose its way and be forced to spend the night in wandering. The air was full of noises that sounded strangely like the stealthy footfall of a tiger and the high grasses on either side of their chairs easily might have concealed some lurking beast ready to spring on its prey.

After an hour of very slow progress, the company reached a group of huts; here the men procured straw torches which were nearly as long as themselves. These torches burned brightly, so that from that time forward their speed materially quickened. The ladies were too deep in thought of what might happen in the future to pay much heed to their surroundings, but a Rembrandt would have delighted in the scene. The lights from the torches threw the figures of the coolies and their burdens into high relief, while the mists obscured everything but a bit of the road ahead. The villages, as they approached, would gradually take on shape and the little twinkling lights with the bright fire from the forge showed the thatched roofs and the quaint outlines of the houses, but fortunately failed to reveal the prevailing squalor.

The first glimpse which the friends caught of the city made them exclaim with surprise and horror, for from many quarters high flames were ascending and columns of smoke filled the heated air with the smell of burning wood.

"What has happened? Who has set the town on fire?" gasped Hsie Yin to Lao Pong.

"Those are bonfires to keep away the sickness, and they are also burning the clothes of the dead. The official has ordered this done on every street," he replied.

"Is the cholera so very bad?" she asked.

"Very, very bad," he answered. "Every family has its victim."

As the party drew yet nearer to their home, they caught the sound of tom-toms and the beating of drums and the boom of the temple bells that were to frighten away the demons that caused the illness; added to these noises were the wailing of mourners and the moans of the dying.

Hsie Yin little realized how accustomed she was to grow to such sounds in the coming weeks, and she only thought to herself, "Surely, this, too, is the call of the East."

## The Deadly Pestilence

When the ladies finally arrived at their compound, a faint glimmer of what was before them began to dawn on their minds. They found every available spot in the wards taken, and the doctor so busy that he could scarcely take time to greet them. Neither of the two women thought of sleep although the doctor urged them to snatch a few hours' rest before they began their work.

"It is bound to last a month at least," he assured them; "I have never known the cholera to get such a foothold in so short a time. Last week I had a few cases which I did not tell you about for fear it would needlessly alarm you. I immediately notified the officials, and sent them some posters which I had prepared, describing how to prevent and treat the disease. I also asked the officials to forbid the sale of melons and all unripe fruit, and not to allow the people from this city to trade with other near-by towns or villages. The head Tao Tai [official] has consented to the notices' being posted on the city gates, but as for stopping the sale of fruit, that would ruin the fruit-sellers' trade and could not be thought of. The restriction of traffic was an other foolish foreign notion; the outside places must look out for themselves."

A strenuous time now began for those in charge of the hospital. They had scarcely time to eat and sleep, and for whole days together they could not undress but threw themselves on their beds to catch just enough repose to keep them alive. Many cases were saved by means of a remedy which had been recently discovered but which took much time and strength to administer. In this way patients coming to them in a state of collapse were brought back to life. The fame of the two doctors spread like wildfire through the city, and as a result the streets leading to the hospital were choked with the litters of the sick.

The epidemic made no distinctions as to rank; rich and poor alike were stricken. Beautifully embroidered coats were no protection, and some of the ladies who had graced Little Small-Feet's first birthday party were among the afflicted. These women were too prejudiced against anything foreign to call in the doctors, so there was no hope of cure for them.

Lord Chang was panic-stricken and would have gone from the city, but as the epidemic raged throughout the country there was no hope of safety anywhere. He therefore shut himself up in the men's court, and refused to take any of the precautions suggested by the posters, but spent his days in holding camphor to his nose in the approved Chinese fashion.

One day when the disease was at its worst, Wang Dah Mah fell ill and there was no mistaking her symptoms. News of it was brought to her worthy master and he turned white with anger to think that the illness should have had the presumption to enter the noble palace of the Changs and endanger his precious life. He immediately ordered that the amah should be turned out on the street. Lady Chang, who was more humane, spent an hour in entreaty, but he was obdurate.

"You are beside yourself," he answered.

"Shall we allow misfortune to follow us by permitting a servant to die in our house? You know the customs of the family; what our fathers did so we must do; on the streets she must go!"

"The customs of the family of Changs have always been very cruel," thought Lady Chang to herself, but she was forced to submit.

Lord Chang, however, had reckoned without his son who, when he heard what his father had done, was very angry. He thought of the faithful service Wang Dah Mah had rendered the family these many years, and his heart burned within him. Was she to be rewarded in such a manner? Not if he could do anything to prevent it! He ordered bearers and had his old nurse gently lifted from the street, where she lay in agony, and had her carried to the foreign hospital. The shades of all the ancestors of young Lord Chang must have turned over, each in his appointed place, at this act, for it was not the custom of the Changs to show benevolence.

Wang Dah Mah was too far gone to care where she was taken, or she might even then have raised a protest. Fortunately for her, the name of Lord Chang had such power that everything in the street gave way to her coolies, and before many minutes elapsed she was taken to the woman's ward and was undergoing the necessary treatment, and in the course of a few hours she began to improve and to take in her surroundings. Hsie Yin was too busy to pay particular attention to any one patient and so it happened that Wang Dah Mah had sized the young doctor up long before Little Small-Feet had noticed her old nurse. The amah's impression of the hospital was much like that which Little Small-Feet had received in the City Lying in the Shadow of Purple Mountain. The cleanliness was of course most surprising and also the discipline, but to Wang Dah Mah, fresh from a palace, it seemed a trifle bare. She could not get over her surprise that a Chinese lady would do for her the little services that Little Small-Feet was continually performing; it certainly was not fitting, and yet the doctor acted with so much grace that she did not seem to lose dignity.

After old Wang Dah Mah had been under treatment for a few days, she was able to sit up, and it was then that Hsie Yin began to notice her more closely.

Wang Dah Mah was so very respectable and of such a different type from the other patients that Hsie Yin's curiosity was aroused.

"May I ask your honorable name, and where you are from?" Little Small-Feet inquired one morning.

"My unworthy name is Wang," answered Wang Dah Mah, "and I come from the house of Lord Chang."

Secretly pleased at being noticed by the busy young doctor, the woman was bright enough to realize that had it not been for those clever hands her earthly life would have ended in a city street, so her old prejudices were flying fast. Hsie Yin started at the name of Chang, remembering how Lord Chang and Creeping Sin had kept together on the steamer. Could this woman be a spy of Old Scarred Face?

"Do you know a man by the name of Creeping Sin and a beggar called Old Scarred Face?" she asked of her patient.

"It is not the custom of respectable people to know such characters," answered Wang Dah Mah much offended. The Chinese lady could not be so lovely after all if she spoke of beggars.

Little Small-Feet saw that she had made a mistake; this worthy old woman evidently knew nothing of Lord Chang's relationship with Creeping Sin, and the girl drew a sigh of relief.

"Wang Dah Mah is a beautiful name," Little Small-Feet continued; "I have always loved that name for some reason."

This statement mollified Wang Dah Mah and, as the days went by, her heart warmed more and more to Hsie Yin and she would sing her praises to the other patients.

"Yes, the foreigner is lovely and has the ways of a virtuous woman, as you say, but give me the little doctor; she comes from our own country and knows our customs and see how clever she is! Even the coolies respect her and do as she bids; she is the person for me. But what makes her do all this when she might be married and have an honorable husband and sons that would carry on her name? I must learn more of this doctrine they are always talking about, and see if it will tell me. It has something to do with love, I know; and to love is certainly an excellent thing. I loved Little Small-Feet but she was taken away by evil spirits and that was bad."

Wang Dah Mah was true to her word and set herself zealously to work to learn the secret that had made Hsie Yin and her lady lead a life of sacrifice. The

Wang Dah Mah After She Had Learned The Story That Rested The Heart

amah attended all the services in the chapel and the prayers in the ward, for by this time she was able to walk about, and her mind must have been the good ground told of in the parable, for in an incredibly short time she accepted the teaching.

"It's bound to be true if Dong Hsiao Dje [Dr. Dong] says so, and I know that she is right, because the story rests my heart," Wang Dah Mah often exclaimed. "The kind deeds they do is all the proof I need."

When the amah told the story of how Lord Chang had had her turned into the street, her friends felt that for the present at least it would be impossible for her to return to the palace. At first they suggested that she should stay with some relatives until the scare about the cholera had blown over, but Wang Dah Mah pleaded so earnestly to be allowed to help with the nursing that it was decided that she should remain as matron of the hospital. A person of her respectability would give the foreigners "face" with the better class of patients as nothing else could do.

It was quite amazing how soon Wang Dah Mah made herself indispensable, for there seemed a peculiar bond between her and Hsie Yin that made them understand each other by a look or a gesture and the devotion of the amah to the young doctor was pretty, to see.

"Wang Dah Mah, I must teach you to read," said Hsie Yin one day when the rush of patients had stopped a little.

"Teach me to read, Dong Hsiao Dje? But that is impossible; I am too old," replied the bewildered Wang Dah Mah.

"Older people than you have done it long before now," returned her friend. "Would you not like to read for yourself the gracious story of the Master healing the sick with a touch of the hand?"

"Oh, yes, and the way he praised the humble women who served him. Do you think he could ever say such words to a person like me, who has only begun to try so late in life?" asked the good soul.

"Indeed he will, for you are not the one to blame; you did not know," answered Hsie Yin.

"If it had not been for the cholera, I would not know now Dong Hsiao Dje."

The old woman's face fairly shone with joy at the new hope that had dawned in her life, and as she watched her expression, Hsie Yin thought with a pang how nearly she had missed this moment by accepting a position in another land. She also remembered the number of people who would have died that summer, had she not been there to help. The sacrifice had paid already. Oh, how it had paid!

From that time forward, whenever there was a spare moment, Wang Dah Mah might be seen poring over a book, her mouth screwed up into strange shapes as a laborious finger pointed to each quaint character. As she went about her work she would be heard croning to herself, very much off the key, the Chinese version of "Jesus Loves Me."

In this manner life at the hospital went on, and Hsie Yin and her friends were happy and busy and utterly unconscious of a small cloud, a very small cloud, that was coming up on the horizon; but small clouds sometime portend a hurricane.

The epidemic was waning and people who had been busy caring for the sick now had time to talk and wonder and spread rumors. There were two recent arrivals in the city who were aware of this fact and aching to take advantage of it for their own evil designs. These two people were of course Creeping Sin and Old Scarred Face, who through their network of spies had learned of Little Small-Feet's presence at the hospital. Nothing could have equaled the worthy pair's satisfaction at this information. It was beyond belief that the three people whom they had hunted so long should be in this inland city, far from the protection of other foreigners. Had they been in the north, it would have been different; a punitive expedition might have been sent; but here the accomplices could escape long before the news of trouble could reach the City by the Sea. There was plenty of time to lay their plots; they must work slowly and carefully and have the plan in perfect order before they at tempted to act.

The news that young Lord Chang had taken the amah to the hospital without his father's con sent, and that the young man had been several times in the company of the foreign doctor, furthered their hopes of getting Lord Chang interested in their schemes. Many a night Old Scarred Face spent in the Spider's den in close conference with Creeping Sin. The net that had been spread for years was to be drawn around the victim at last.

As for Lord Chang, he had grown very weary of his enforced isolation in his palace and one day when he received an invitation to a feast from one of his most disreputable acquaintances, he decided that here was an opportunity to relieve his boredom.

The feast proceeded with the usual formalities and observances of etiquette and the conversation was general, but during one of the courses, while the other guests were deep in a discussion, Lord Chang's next neighbor whispered to him:

"Creeping Sin has returned to the city, and he has a scheme he wants to lay before your highness, that he thinks will be of great profit. He will meet you in a place you know of to-morrow evening."

Lord Chang, without changing a muscle of his face to show that he had heard, continued daintily helping himself to a delicate piece of sea slug. This fellow must not think that he, the great Lord Chang, cared one snap of a finger for Creeping Sin and his message.

At this minute a hush fell on the company, so no reply could be made and the feast continued to its end without Lord Chang's speaking again to his neighbor.

The whole of the next day Lord Chang was in two minds about accepting Creeping Sin's invitation. "The man is getting too impudent," he thought, "these affairs should be arranged by go betweens." Still he remembered there were some things too delicate to arrange by such agents; the fewer the people involved in them, the less danger there was of being caught.

In the evening, therefore, he ordered his chair and was carried away. Creeping Sin was too wily to invite a man of Lord Chang's position into the den where he had received Old Scarred Face. He had many haunts throughout the city, and he met no two people in the same place. The nobleman found his host ready and waiting, and the sly man was all obsequiousness and courtesy. There was in his cringing manner that which would have revolted anyone less vain than Lord Chang, but to him such treatment was as the breath of life. The sweetmeats were of the most delicate flavor and the tea had just been brought the day before from the banks of the river Han.

A full hour was consumed in polite nothings and gossip of the city, and not until the opium pipes were brought out and the men began to feel its soothing effects did Creeping Sin turn the conversation toward his object. He first suggested that he wished to borrow money for a friend, and after much bargaining offered such a high rate of interest that Lord Chang was in a great good humor. Then very carefully he engineered the conversation to the subject of the foreigners and their work in the city.

"I feel myself far too unworthy to make suggestions to your highness, but the proverb says that 'where the prince leads the people follow,' and perhaps if some plan was put on foot, we could drive these barbarians away."

"Meddling with foreigners is bad for the health," replied Lord Chang, thinking how heavily his pocketbook had suffered on account of the Boxer movement.

"Your excellency's wisdom is broader than the ocean, yet we all realize that 'strict fathers make filial sons.' It is widely known through the city that the young lord, your noble son, has been seen with the foreign doctor; in fact he is frequently at the hospital and Wang Dah Mah, the old amah, was treated there for cholera. Does it seem strange that the impression is being spread that you are smiling on the foreigners with your august favors?" As he asked this question, Creeping Sin watched Lord Chang very keenly.

Needless to say no such impression was abroad; the relations between Lord Chang and his son were very well known in the city, and the fact that Wang Dah Mah had been turned out in the street pretty widely discussed. Lord Chang heard this news with not a change of feature but he nearly bit the stem of his pipe through in his rage. What was the world coming to, that sons were thwarting their fathers behind their backs?

"These rumors are new to me, but if they are correct, something must be done. What would you suggest? If what I hear is true, you are not wanting in resources. Why do you come to me?" Lord Chang replied.

"'Where the prince leads the people follow' was ever a wise proverb. Lord Chang's reputation is not bounded by the seas; he is known to the ends of the earth." Creeping Sin's compliment was not idle, for Lord Chang's name had been discussed in every cabinet in Europe and America at the time of the Boxer uprising.

"Names are not safe tools to use," replied the nobleman with a threatening scowl. "There are others beside mine that are well known."

"Your wisdom is as deep and wide as the Pacific Ocean; discretion is always the wisest course; it is easy enough to start a rumor of poisoned wells and strange incantations. A little cash wisely spent oils the wheels in such cases, and this time the barbarians must be exterminated; no halfway measures ever drive out vermin. It would be worth the price to hire men to do it."

"My purse is as clean as though it had been washed; I could contribute only what is a patch under the armpit to complete a whole jacket," answered Lord Chang. "How much is desired?"

"Your excellency is generous, as always," responded Creeping Sin with a ceremonious bow.

For the remainder of the evening, the two conspirators haggled over "price" and who should hire the assassins. Creeping Sin wished the nobleman to do the negotiating with the criminals, hoping in this way to get him more deeply involved in the affair, but he was unsuccessful and was forced to be contented with Lord Chang's offer to contribute part of the bribe.

"I will have some hidden witnesses when he pays the money; it will amount to the same thing," thought the Spider.

The final farewells were said and the guest bowed out, and then Creeping Sin clapped his hands, and from an inner apartment Old Scarred Face and a man appeared.

"Well, old hag, you have heard the talk, are you satisfied with the result?" asked Creeping Sin with his slanting look and horrid grin.

"May all our enemies be as much in our power as that purse-proud lord!" she answered.

The night was passed by the trio in completing the plot and hiring their accomplices; for thoroughness of detail, nothing could surpass the combined powers of Old Scarred Face and Creeping Sin. They were absolutely certain that this time no earthly power should balk them of their prey.

# Chapter XI
# "The Terror By Night"

Be a good soldier, and a guardian just;
Likewise an upright judge, Let no one thrust
You in a dubious cause to testify
Through fear of tyrant's vengeance to a lie.
Count it is baseness if your soul prefer
Safety above what honor asks of her!
And hold it manly, life itself to give,
Rather than lose the things for which we live.

—*Eighth Satire of Juvenal,*
Translated By Henry Van Dyke.

When the bright, sunny days and cool, bracing nights of autumn came, the epidemic began to subside throughout the city and the citizens resumed their everyday occupations. There were many gaps among them, however, and scores of new graves to be wailed over out on the hillside.

The tide of prejudice which had set so strongly against the foreigners had now turned and ran the other way, and the hospital received many presents of long lacquered boards, covered with highly complimentary characters, to hang in its reception room. The Sunday services in the street chapels were crowded and the wards and clinics were also full of patients suffering from he most unusual complaints.

"Their suspicions have been overcome at last!" exclaimed Little Small-Feet joyfully. "In the street I am always treated with respect. They have found out, as you did, that foreign ways are kind. Have they not, Wang Dah Mah?"

"Yes, Dong Hsiao Dje, I have learned many things and I am ashamed to think how small my heart was when I first found myself within these walls. But all is not so pleasant as you think; no good ever comes to foreigners in a city where Lord Chang resides. I wish the young Lord Chang would be discreet; if it comes to his father's ears how he haunts the foreign doctor, you may all be turned out from the city. Be ware a serpent or a tiger " warned Wang Dah Mah.

"He should be more careful," the girl replied, "but the doctor teaches him many things he longs to know, and he is so much safer here than among the temptations in his father's palace; it seems impossible to ask him to stay away."

"If he loses his life and yours, too, it may be a mistaken kindness to allow him to come," Wang Dah Mah insisted.

"How about yourself, Wang Dah Mah? Is Lord Chang overjoyed to have you here?" inquired Hsie Yin.

"I have been forbidden ever to cross the threshold of his house again; I am sorry, for I want to tell my mistress about the gracious message of peace for the weary, and she needs it, for these are stormy days in the house of Chang," and with a deep sigh Wang Dah Mah returned to her book.

At about the same hour when Hsie Yin was talking so hopefully, a group of the city women were down at the river's bank doing their family washing. Their stooping posture did not seem to make it necessary for them to hold their tongues, and they discussed with relish every morsel of gossip they had heard that day. They were so engrossed with their conversation that they did not hear a water coolie stop beside them until he began to fill his buckets.

"Do you draw water from the river, when that from the city wells is so much cooler?" asked a woman greatly surprised.

"I dare not use those springs for the 'foreign devils' have poisoned them and caused the sickness," he replied.

"Poisoned our wells!" the women exclaimed in chorus. "What tale is this you bring?"

"No tale at all but the very truth; I heard it from the mouth of the man whose neighbor's first cousin saw them do it."

Here was news, indeed, of a variety that would make a fine stir! Life was growing monotonous; now there would be something to discuss in the courtyards of an afternoon. Poor old Li Sao Tze, the blind woman who had been cured by Hsie Yin, was the only one to doubt it.

"There must be some mistake," she cried; "the foreigners are benevolent; they would not do such a dreadful thing! I ought to know for they gave me back my sight. They were away when the sickness came; how could they have brought it? They tried to cure those who were ill. It would be a foolish thing to take the trouble to poison people and then make them well! Dui Sao Tze, they raised your son from the dead, how can you believe these idle stories?"

"Who can explain the ways of 'foreign devils'!" the man retorted. "Our priests all say that we meddle with them at our own risks. In the dead of night the foreign doctor was seen to throw a fine gray powder into the well, at which a smoke, smelling strongly of brimstone, arose and hid the spot. The people ran to the place but all that they could see was the well, looking much as usual, but from the rear of some houses came a dreadful laugh and the earth shook at the sound. The next day the illness broke out and of course nothing could stop it until the demons had chosen whom they would to accompany them into the shades. The officials did what they could and had the south gate shut for a month, when it was most inconvenient, to keep the heat out as it came up from the south and to prevent it from entering the city, but closing city gates has no effect after the demons have gotten in."

"We remember that the city gates were shut, and it was as he says, the heat grew hotter and hotter and greater and greater until our very flesh dried up, and the sickness increased with the heat. It is more than plain, the officials did their duty, but what chance had they against the wily barbarians?" continued Li Sao Tze's neighbor, who had been rather jealous of the blind woman's famous cure.

Having told his story, the man took up his water buckets and returned to the city, stopping here and there to recount his gossip. The rumor spread with amazing rapidity, and as it spread the story grew and the feeling against the foreigners grew with it. The patients who had been at the hospital did their best to stop slanderous tongues, but they were a mere handful compared to the ignorant multitude.

The City of the Blue Pagoda had the reputation of being the most conservative town in the whole of the Empire. A dragon was reported to lie buried in a high mound outside the great walls. Several hundred years ago a series of earthquake shocks had made it apparent that although the monster was properly interred he was not really dead, and that he had grown restless where he lay. The blue pagoda was therefore built on the top of the grave to keep the creature as quiet as possible. This clever scheme had been highly successful, as the oldest living inhabitant could tell, and the dragon moved now only at rare intervals when some occurrence in the city did not please him. Unfortunately, at this moment he chose to give a shake, and his activity was the final event which threw the suspicious people into a panic. It was not a vicious jar; it might have been termed a gentle hint; but the rough element in the city were in a mood to heed a very gentle hint.

The ladies themselves were too busy to pay attention to the vague rumors Wang Dah Mah brought to them. There is always gossip and prejudice in a

Chinese community, and if foreigners stopped work every time they heard an uncomplimentary report, there would be little accomplished. They did observe, however, that there was a great falling off in the attendance at the hospital and the street services were nearly deserted, but they were philosophical about it, for they realized that popularity is a fickle dame.

The night of the earthquake they hardly felt the tremor, for there were several very ill patients in the ward and a serious operation was proceeding. Wang Dah Mah noticed the tremble with much misgiving and spent a restless, unhappy night.

When one lies awake in the darkness, fears seem very wise, indeed, but when a clear autumn sun shines on us, the apprehensions seem needless and silly. Wang Dah Mah arose the next day with the firm intention of persuading her friends to leave the vicinity for a time, but everything looked so bright and cheerful and Hsie Yin greeted her with such careless gayety that she chided herself for having these forebodings.

"It would be sad indeed for me if the foreigners went away," she thought.

As the hours passed on, both the doctors were called out to visit patients on the other side of the city. Hsie Yin felt that by this time it was safe to go without an escort, and started forth in her chair with her usual bearers. She perceived, however, that when she gave her orders to the coolies, they laughed in her face in a disrespectful manner, and murmured to themselves a word that sounded like "friend of the foreign devil." On her way home some little street gamins threw stones at her and when she told the bearers to go faster, they only went more slowly. Looking through the window at the back of her chair, she saw a small crowd collecting and their looks were black indeed. Among the number was Dui Sao Tze and one or two other women whom she recognized. The young doctor insisted that the men halt and, stepping down from her chair, she turned and faced the rabble.

"Dui Sao Tze, what are you doing here?" she exclaimed in a stern voice. "Is this the manner of gratitude taught by the sages? Do you not know that your son would be a dead man to-day if it had not been for the hospital? Does he know where you are?"

Dui Sao Tze looked ashamed: "The gods are angry at you. They sent the earthquake to show their displeasure that we have allowed 'foreign devils' to dwell among us."

"Have you no understanding? If the gods, as you believe, take note of what is going on around them, they are probably angry at the ungrateful way you are treating the people who tried to help you when you were ill!" Hsie Yin replied. "Did it ever strike you that your gods disapproved of the way you listened to the evil counsels of Old Scarred Face and Creeping Sin?"

This struck home and the more respectable of the people turned away and disappeared in various directions.

"She has spoken wisely," said an old woman in the front; "Old Scarred Face never did a kind deed in her life; her ways are always evil."

Hsie Yin had made a happy guess when she spoke of Old Scarred Face, for Wang Dah Mah, who knew little of Hsie Yin's history, had failed to mention the fact of the beggar's return.

The crowd having dispersed, Hsie Yin climbed into her chair and was carried by her subdued coolies to the hospital. She found on her arrival that the foreign doctor had returned after a very similar experience, but he had not been able to throw off the crowd of rowdies and they had followed him to the very gate of the hospital. Pastor Meng had come and he and Wang Dah Mah both looked very anxious.

"This earthquake is most unfortunate; the people are always restless and apprehensive at such times, and Old Scarred Face is at work; we may always look for trouble when she is near. I think that it would be wiser for all of you to slip quietly out of the city after nightfall and take refuge in the mountains until the trouble passes over," said Pastor Meng.

"What he says is wise and sensible," affirmed Wang Dah Mah. "It is the only thing to do."

"Could we not send to the yamen for a guard?" asked the Great Helpful Lady. "If there is a riot, it may get the Tao Tai into trouble and he will lose his position."

"Unfortunately he is in the power of Lord Chang, but perhaps it would be as well. It would make them both responsible for an uprising," said Pastor Meng.

"I do not see how we can leave," faltered Hsie Yin. "Think of the two women we operated on last night; they will die if they do not have proper care."

"Tell me what to do, Dong Hsiao Dje!" pleaded Wang Dah Mah. "No one is looking for me, and my fingers are not so clumsy but what I can keep the wounds dressed."

Then the conference closed and very calmly, as though no storm was brewing, they all went about their particular duties. The soldiers were sent for, and the official who kept the city gates was paid to keep the nearest gate open until after midnight. It was decided that late in the evening they would slip away through a gate in the rear of the compound.

"I would never consider doing such a thing," said the foreign doctor, "if I didn't feel that we should imperil the lives of our helpers by remaining. Pastor Meng would never think of his own safety and would stick to us until the bitter end. What makes the matter more serious is the fact that I feel certain that Creeping Sin and Old Scarred Face are at the bottom of the trouble. We know from past experience how absolutely unscrupulous they are and to what methods they resort."

The dragon under the blue pagoda seemed to have joined in the popular feeling against the foreigners, for late in the afternoon there came a rumble and then a roar and the city was shaken to its very foundations. Tiles fell from roofs and plaster walls crumbled like paper. The wonder was that many people were not killed; although a number were cut by flying debris, one small boy was the only victim. Excitement rose to fever heat all over the town, and neighbors ran to the parents of the dead child and told them that all their children would suffer the same fate if the foreigners were not driven out.

"The dragon," cried the coolie, "is very angry at our delay; we have been too kind-hearted and we must suffer for it."

As night began to fall the temper of the people grew more ugly, and a murmur like that of an angry beehive arose from many streets. At seven Pastor Meng hastened to the hospital.

"There is no use in waiting; there will be no quiet in the city to-night. You had better get away at once. The back gate is watched, but our next neighbors have been friendly ever since you cured the wife. They say that you may climb over the wall into their garden and escape through the side door that opens on a side street. You must all put on Chinese garments and as you love your life do not speak!"

"Pastor Meng, do leave us at once. We can take care of ourselves, and you must remember your wife and family. We have persuaded Wang Dah Mah to visit friends, for with her bound feet she could not stand the walking. Do go while there is time!" pleaded the Great Helpful Lady.

"The patients have all been taken away by their relatives and that is a very bad sign. My family went this afternoon, and as for myself I could not leave the best friends I have in the world to the mercy of the mob. That is not the way I learned the doctrine. Anyway it is now too late. Listen!" answered Pastor Meng.

As he finished speaking there was a great pounding on the front gate and a sound of cat calls and curses. The crowd had stolen forward quietly on their cloth shoes in order to make a surprise attack, and now the street at the front of the compound was seething with people.

"Quickly! Quickly! Quickly go! Take the ladder and climb the wall and I will hide it!" exclaimed the evangelist.

At that moment Lao Pong, the faithful servant, appeared. He had been absent all day and they thought that he had run away, but now he adjusted the ladder and assisted the ladies to climb the wall, while the kindly neighbor helped them on the other side. Then Lao Pong let the ladder down to the waiting Meng Sien Sung and followed the foreigners.

"I came back because I thought you might need me," he explained. "At first I thought I would seek a safe place but afterwards I knew that was showing a poor disposition, so here I am."

Instead of accompanying the others, Pastor Meng deliberately hid the ladder and then turned toward the compound gateway.

"If I can keep the crowd talking, it will give them a better chance to escape," he thought.

At that moment the first of the mob burst through the gate and the yelling, hooting rabble rushed into the compound.

"What are you doing here?" Pastor Meng boldly said to the ringleaders. "Are you not afraid to molest foreign property? Remember the Boxer movement and the taxes we are paying at this moment on account of it; everything destroyed may have to be returned. Then there will be no rice in your bowls." He noticed as he spoke that the soldiers from the yamen were mingled with the others and he knew then that the matter was very serious.

The crowd seemed a little abashed and fell back a moment at the preacher's courageous words.

"He seems to speak with reason," said a few of the better class, who, carried away by the excitement caused by the earthquake, had joined the tumult.

"Remember the dead child; we shall all be like him if we let the foreigners remain," shouted a voice in the rear that had the accents of Old Scarred Face. "Clear the foreigners out; death to the foreigners, I say!"

Other voices took up the cry and rushed through the hospital. If Pastor Meng had been one whit less brave, he would have slipped away in the confusion, but he thought only of saving the compound from burning. He therefore went with the others and watched the looting of the houses. Every inch of ground was searched but no trace of the foreigners could be found; then, fairly foaming with disappointment, the leaders turned on the evangelist.

"Where are the foreigners gone? They must have flown through the air by their enchantments for we had both gates watched!"

"If you think them as clever as that I do not see why you ever hoped to catch them," retorted Pastor Meng, for every minute he could keep the mob in the compound might mean life to his friends. "I should think you would be afraid to meddle with people who could go and come unseen. It does not seem very safe."

"The man knows where they are and he is trying to keep us from finding them," yelled the water coolie. "If we hang him to the doorpost, he will tell quite enough."

"Speak, speak, or we will kill you!" screamed the mob. "Renounce the strange doctrine and give the foreigners up, or you are a dead man!"

Pastor Meng looked this way and that, but he was surrounded by a sea of hostile faces. The better element in the crowd had disappeared at the threat of bloodshed and those who were left, hardened with superstitious fear, were thirsting for vengeance. There was no help.

An exalted look swept over the pastor's face; it verily seemed to shine. His lips moved as if in prayer and with a ringing voice he exclaimed:

"I will not tell you where the foreigners are because they are the best friends I have ever had, and the best friends this city has! Years ago when I was dying of cholera, they took me into their hospital and nursed me back to life. Should I be false to them now? That is not the idea of gratitude the ancients taught us. I am not afraid for"—and his voice took on a note of triumph—"I believe in God, the Father Almighty, and in Jesus Christ, his only Son, our Lord!" At the first words the rioters listened breathless, astonished at the man's courage; then someone moved and the spell was broken. A hand threw a stone that caught the pastor on the forehead and he fell headlong. A soldier near, as if to complete the mischief, stabbed him with a knife. One of the crowd, with more feeling than the rest, saw the lips of the dying man move and stooping over caught his last words:

"Oh, I see Jesus, I see Jesus," he whispered, and then the brave heart stopped beating. Pastor Meng had freely laid down his life rather than betray his friends and lose the truth for which he had lived.

The crowd surged forward again and with their fierce cries awakened the echoes.

"Slay the 'foreign devils'! Slay the 'foreign devils'!" they shrieked.

At that moment a man came running up the street and entering the compound asked for the water coolie.

"The foreigners have left the city by the gate of the blue pagoda; they are probably going to the Fearsome Caverns," the man shouted. "If they reach there they will let loose all the demons that haunt the caves, and the shaking of the dragon will be as nothing to the ill that will then befall the city."

At these words the mob turned and started for the great gates on a mad run. A few only remained behind to complete the looting of the hospital, and afterwards dispersed to their homes.

The Fearsome Caverns were names to conjure within the city, for they went far into the mountain side and were full of passages and underground rooms. Mammoth bats hung to the ceiling and blind fish were to be found in a stream that gurgled and spluttered through one section of the grotto. A single call would awake the echoes that would thunder down the passages for several moments, and cries and groans were often heard issuing from the mouth of the cave. It was no wonder that rumor reported that no animal, not even a dog, ever entered this place and returned alive, and heaps of bones at the entrance confirmed this superstition. The boldest citizen would hesitate to enter these black depths alone in the daytime and the man who would attempt to do so at night would be considered insane. For reasons of their own the ruffians of the neighborhood had done their best to spread such stories and the place was the resort of all the wild characters throughout the Province. All these things made it seem wiser to catch the fugitives before they gained their shelter.

When the rioters reached the city gate the country without looked so forbidding that many were for turning back and waiting for the morning to continue their search, but others snatched up torches and lanterns and still crying vengeance upon the barbarians dashed forward into the murky night. Then at length Old Scarred Face threw all caution to the winds, for up to this moment she had kept herself rather in the background, and from this time forward led the pursuit.

In the meantime the refugees had, as reported, headed for the caverns. Lao Pong was invaluable, and from the moment that they had climbed the wall he had taken command. He showed great skill in leading them down unfrequented lanes and out-of-the-way alleys, telling them when to move and when to remain motionless under the shadow of a building or overhanging balcony. He finally brought them into a court yard a short distance within the city gates and here they found chairs waiting for them provided by the young Lord Chang, for Lao Pong had seen him early in the evening and, knowing that he could be trusted, had told him of the expected flight and had arranged with the young man to have the chairs in readiness.

Lord Chang's son was no coward and at the risk of his life he met the foreigners at the courtyard and begged to be allowed to accompany them on their flight, feeling sure that his great name would give them much protection. His brave offer was refused and he had to content himself with giving them a card to use at the gate which would keep them from dangerous delay. Fortunately, this card worked like magic and the soldiers allowed them to pass without a question. The fugitives kept the curtains of their chairs carefully closed, however, and Lao Pong represented them as friends of the young nobleman who were fleeing from the earthquake.

When the blue pagoda was reached it was determined to send back the chairs, as there was grave question as to the loyalty of the bearers, and it was thought wiser to proceed alone. Thus Lao Pong again showed his sagacity, for it was one of these very men who reported to the water coolie their presence at the blue pagoda.

Fortunately, the foreigners had a long start of the rioters, and they had gone far into the depths of the caverns before their pursuers reached the entrance. Here at length the crowd paused in their headlong progress. The most part were for giving it up and returning to the city; others wished to place a guard and thus starve their victims out. Old Scarred Face, true to her character, scorned such weak counsels.

"You cows," she shouted, "you are just old women; of course you are afraid, but I have a charm here"—and she held a charm high above her head—"that will save all who enter with the righteous intention of ridding this Province forever from the taint of the foreigner.

"Who are the immortals who will go with me?" she cried, as the crowd still faltered.

"She is the witch of the cavern; we will be safe enough with her," called the water coolie who had been well paid to impart this knowledge.

A few of the wavering turned back, but the rest with hoots and howls ran on into the dark cave.

# Chapter XII

# The Fearsome Caverns

> Down a corridor dark as death,
> With beating hearts and bated breath
> We hurried; far away we heard
> A dreadful hissing, fierce as fire
> When rain begins to quench a pyre;
> And where the smoky torch-light flared
> Strange vermin beat their bat-like wings,
> And the wet wall dropped with slimy things.
>
> —Alfred Noyes.

Many poets have written and many minstrels have sung praises to the beauties of the night—night with its thousand stars and myriad eyes, night with its silvery moonlight and soft breezes that caress the cheek. But if one wishes to realize the terrors that the midnight hours can hold, one must turn to the songs of the old Hebrew bards. They portray impartially both the glories and the horrors of darkness, and this goes far to explain their hold on the imagination of every race, for they speak the language of a common experience.

When the little party of refugees plunged down the dark galleries of the Fearsome Caverns, pursued by pitiless and relentless foes, they felt to the very marrow of their bones what "the terror by night" might mean. As they entered the mouth of the cave they could hear from far away the voices of their pursuers and see the glimmer of their lanterns. The foreign doctor had a tiny electric flash light, and by its rays they found the way. Lao Pong had heard there was a subterranean river running through the den and he felt that near it they might find a hiding place. They stumbled along over stones and around huge rocks, never daring to speak or whisper, although the road seemed endless and sometimes they feared that they were but going around in a circle, for in the dim shadows they seemed to recognize objects which they had passed before. The ladies were almost exhausted and frequently had to pause for rest. At length the party reached a long corridor-like alley where they could stand erect; up to this time they had been forced to run in a stooping position. Ahead of them they thought that they recognized the murmur of a stream, when suddenly they heard a shout of triumph and, turning, saw behind them the lanterns of their pursuers. The cries that went up from the mob froze their blood and made their hearts almost stand still, but terror gave new strength to their dragging feet and they darted forward. When the friends reached the river, they found that a narrow footpath ran beside it and they instinctively followed it.

"We must go across to that opening on the other side; there is a hole or well not far from there where we may be able to hide until they are weary and give up the search," whispered Lao Pong.

"Is it very deep?" asked the ladies.

"I do not know," replied Lao Pong, "but it is better to drown than to fall into the hands of Old Scarred Face."

Holding tightly to one another's hands, the fugitives went into the torrent. Each step brought them into deeper water and the current ran very swiftly, but they did not falter although they often tripped over loose stones. The water rose to their knees and then to their waists and to their shoulders; the next step promised to bring them beyond their depth; but, no, the stream was growing lower, and they at length could stand dripping and shivering on the other bank. They dared not pause, however, and turning they crawled on hands and knees through a narrow passage that admitted only one person at a time. The foreign doctor went first, then the ladies followed, and Lao Pong brought up the rear.

The passage terminated suddenly in a drop of about twelve feet. When the doctor first used his light in it, he thought that the pit was unfathomable; it looked as if they would be forced to return and face their enemies or die miserably like rats in a hole. On closer examination, however, he thought that he could see the bottom, but it was full of water. Would it be beyond his depth? About halfway down the wall of the cavern he saw a slight projection that might give him foothold. Only a desperate person would have attempted the descent, but he decided to try. He removed his coat and handing it to his wife told her to grasp it firmly and he would hold on to the other end to steady himself, then very carefully he let himself down to the tiny shelf; this he reached in safety, and could see the water only a few feet below him. There was nothing to do but jump, trusting that the pool was not too deep. His lips moved in silent prayer; then he leaped into the darkness. To his relief he found the water only up to his knees, so he whispered of his safety to his anxious wife. He then gave her minute instructions how to follow him, standing ready to catch her should she slip. Thus one after another they scrambled down into their moist retreat.

Lao Pong very cautiously explored their hiding place but could find no other outlet into the cavern; they therefore decided to hide themselves behind the huge bowlders at the farther end, trusting that their pursuers would give up the hunt rather than attempt the perilous descent into the hole.

Meanwhile there was division in the camp of their enemies. They had turned the corner of the passageway just too late to see their victims ford the river and plunge into the gallery on the other bank. When the crowd had reached the place where the party had crossed the stream, the leaders were uncertain which road to take. Some wished to dash right in, but others felt that it was wiser to keep themselves and their clothes dry by remaining on the path on which they were.

"Only fools would leap into a river when there was another path to follow," said the water coolie. "It is too cold a night and too far from the city to wet oneself to the skin."

"You are the foolish one to think in such a manner," replied Old Scarred Face. "The 'foreign devils' knew how afraid you cowards are of a little dampness and that is the very reason they would cross the stream."

"You can swim over if you like, Old Tiger," answered the man. "I for one shall take the other road," and off he started followed by the others.

Old Scarred Face ground her teeth at the thought of losing such precious time, but she did not dare to go over alone; so she was forced to give in. The rioters spent a full hour in searching corridors and alleys, but not a trace of the fugitives could they find.

"They are demons, indeed, and have gone to their own place," said the coolie. "How could we mere human beings hope to find them? I think that it is prudent to return to the city; we have banished them and they will never be bold enough to return. We have probably lost all the loot by coming away as we did, and who will say that we have been wise?"

At these words the mob started on a wild run to the entrance, but Old Scarred Face came close beside the coolie.

"Not one cash will Creeping Sin give you unless you bring the hair of the foreigners to show that they are dead," the woman threatened.

This caused the coolie to halt; to lose the loot and the bribe as well would be to lose everything.

"Old Scarred Face says that she saw the barbarians cross the river," he shouted. "Let us go back and hunt for them on the other side; we should lose face if we returned to the city with our task unfinished. All who slay foreigners acquire merit that covers millions of sins."

At these words the crowd retraced their steps and were soon on the banks of the stream. With much cursing and reviling, they plunged into the river and struggled to the other side. Again a controversy ensued whether to crawl into the narrow passageway or take a path that followed the torrent. Old Scarred Face finally prevailed and led them down the gallery. The crowd had been careless of their lanterns and torches in the crossing and these had gotten wet and gone out; in consequence they only had one feeble lantern which Old Scarred Face carried. When she came to the deep hole, she held the light well over the brink and the flickering rays lighted up her withered, scowling features, so that the fugitives cowering in a distant corner could see it vividly. Even the old woman's bravado shrank at the depth of that pit and the water at its bottom.

"It is a bad place," she called back to the others, "without a ladder or ropes it would not be safe to attempt it. If the foreign devils are there, they can never escape for they cannot climb up that sheer wall. We have them in a trap at last."

Since their leader was in this mood, the others were not loath to retire; they were cold "and the first excitement of the chase was over, so they hurried as fast as they could to the mouth of the cavern.

Old Scarred Face was about to leave the cave when a restraining hand was put on her arm and she was dragged back into the shadow. Turning, she looked up into the face of her fellow conspirator, Creeping Sin.

"How goes it; are the barbarians dead?" he inquired eagerly.

"No! May eagles eat their hearts out! They escaped but I think I know where they lie hidden, and I will take you there so that we can plan how best to get them," she answered.

"Bungler, as usual!" he taunted. "Your well laid plots are clumsy; I wonder I use such a blunt tool."

"Bungler! Indeed!" the woman exclaimed.

"How about the voyage on the Pacific, and the trap you laid in that distant city where the girl was educated? What are you, to speak of bunglers?"

Creeping Sin saw that the woman was wet and tired and in no mood to be baited, so he let the matter drop, but he eyed her malignantly as she strode ahead of him.

"She is growing old; all her schemes fall through; she knows more than is convenient of my past; I must shortly get rid of her," he thought to himself.

The two conspirators crossed the stream, and crept down the narrow gallery; at the end Old Scarred Face stopped and pointed out to Creeping Sin, who peered eagerly over her shoulder, the sheer rocky wall and the water below. A sudden impulse seized the man: What better place could he find to do away with his enemy! No one would connect his name with this spot! At that moment Old Scarred Face leaned far out over the edge, for she thought that she saw something moving at the farther end of the hole. Creeping Sin drew back a little to give force to his blow and then with all his strength pushed her over the brink.

With a wild shriek the woman fell to the bottom; the water splashed high; then all was still. Old Scarred Face had carried the lantern so Creeping Sin had no light and was obliged to feel his way back to the river.

"One witness less to my past career," he thought. "If the foreigners are in that place, they will starve to death; they cannot possibly climb that wall; so we need not trouble more about them. I wish all my enemies were likely to give me as little trouble."

Hardly waiting to be sure that Creeping Sin had permanently disappeared, the foreign doctor moved cautiously forward to rescue Old Scarred Face from what promised to be a watery grave. He must take no risks, however, for she might return to consciousness and raise an outcry. By means of his electric flash light, he soon located her. She had fallen in a shallow place with her head against a rock that just raised her mouth above the water. If she had struck a foot either way, she would certainly have been drowned.

Carefully he lifted the woman and carried her to a flat rock near the center of the hole and then began his examination. His wife watched Hsie Yin with interest, for the test had come at last of which they had spoken so long ago. Would the younger woman offer to help, or would she allow the foreign doctor to do the work alone?

Without a moment's hesitation, Little Small-Feet stepped forward and went to the doctor's side.

"Let me assist you," she said simply.

The woman still remained unconscious but in a few minutes they were able to determine partially the extent of the damage. Her head was terribly bruised and her arm broken and a rib fractured; they suspected also that some injury had been done to the spine, but at present it was impossible to tell how much. The ladies tore their skirts into strips to make bandages for the patient and they bound her up as well as they could with the few means at hand. The next problem was how to leave the cave, for a day and a night spent in the cold watery cavern would mean death to them all. It seemed absolutely impossible to scale the wall, and if they could manage it themselves they certainly could not raise the unconscious woman to the passage above.

While the friends were consulting what to do, Lao Pong had borrowed the light from the doctor and began to go carefully around their prison to see what he could find. Suddenly he gave a low exclamation of pleasure and began to remove some large stones heaped up in one corner.

"What have you found?" whispered the doctor.

"I am not sure, but it seems like another corridor which leads directly out into the open air," answered Lao Pong.

This news seemed too good to be true, and with feverish haste they began to help him. The floor of the cave sloped up to this spot, and although it was damp and slippery the water did not stand here. They found that the stones which blocked the entrance had been piled up from the outside. Two huge bowlders which stood a foot or so away on the inside of their prison had kept them from noticing the character of this pile of stones.

Before many minutes the passageway was quite free and Lao Pong stole stealthily to the farther end to find out how the land lay. The first faint flickering of light showed that the dawn was not far distant; if they wished to hide elsewhere, they must hurry. The faithful servant cautiously moved the bushes that grew thick around the entrance and seeing no lights or signs of human habitation he felt his way carefully along a narrow pathway. It was evident that he had come out on the other side of the mountain from the city, for here was no view of the blue pagoda or the river but only a long, deep valley, hedged in with mountain peaks. Suddenly it occurred to him that he had blundered on the place called the Spirit Valley, and somewhere in the distance he saw the dim outline of a building which he felt must be a ruined temple. All sorts of wild rumors were circulated about this place. Long ago a priest had been murdered here and since then no Chinese, rich or poor, good or bad, no matter how desperate, had dared enter the precincts. Lao Pong himself shook with fear; nevertheless, he hurried to the very walls of the building and found as he had conjectured that it was the temple which he sought. No sound was to be heard but the dismal hoot of an owl from an old tree, and when its notes struck on Lao Pong's ears, he took to his heels and ran at he top of his speed to the cavern.

The little party were delighted with his report for he could not have found a safer spot for a hiding place. Without more ado they started for the temple, Lao Pong and the foreign doctor carrying Old Scarred Face, who though very tall was nothing but skin and bones, and no weight to strong men. It never seemed to occur to them that they might leave her to her fate as Creeping Sin had done.

The shelter of the temple was a great protection from the cold winds that blew just before the dawn. They found a room in the rear of the big idol where the priests had lived. Lao Pong gathered some dry branches and made a small fire at which they dried themselves, but as soon as the sun showed behind a distant peak they were forced to put out the blaze for fear it would betray them.

At night the Spirit Valley was always deserted, because no peasant or traveling merchant would risk its enchantments in the darkness, but in the daytime the thrifty farmers could not bear to let so much good land lie idle, so the hillside was covered with little plots of cultivated ground. A road ran through one end of the glen and over a high pass to the neighboring market town. In broad daylight this road was much frequented by merchants, but these worthy men of business were very careful not to be caught there as evening fell.

Throughout the whole of the following day the friends had to content themselves with staying strictly within the shelter of the temple walls. Without food or drink their lot was pitiable in deed, and the groans of the wounded woman in the corner and her moaning for water added much to their distress. At times they feared lest some passing peasant might hear her shrieks but the reputation of their retreat kept them safe from prying eyes and the screams only added to the evil character of the place.

Above the room in which they crouched was a loft full of broken idols, old sacks, and straw matting. The foreign doctor brought down the latter to make rough beds for the ladies and the sick woman, and throughout the long hours they rested from the fatigue of the preceding evening. The doctor felt that if they should be spied upon by any marauders they could retire to the loft and set up such heart-rending shrieks and groan that no one would suspect that the dignified foreigners had taken refuge there.

The sun sparkled brightly, and the valley lay basking in its peaceful rays; on the temple walls doves billed and cooed and pruned their soft plumage; it was hard to realize that a few li away there was a mob that was panting for their lives. Once late in the afternoon a band of ragged men went down the road calling and beating stocks and their words resounded among the hills.

"Death to the foreign devils," they shouted.

"Slay the barbarians!" and the echoes took up their cry and prolonged it dreadfully.

The farmers, working their tiny fields, ran to hear what was the matter, and they joined in the shouts until the air rang with them. Then the crowd separated and searched through all the underbrush and groves of trees, but they gave the temple a wide berth, for they would run no risks where it was concerned. Old Scarred Face and her charm had mysteriously disappeared, and anyway her charm had not saved them a terrible wetting the night before; they shivered now when they thought of it.

When night came on Lao Pong stole out to forage for food. In the fields he found some late turnips and carrots and under a chestnut tree some delicious nuts. In the corner under a ruined stable he discovered a nest of a truant hen and stole the hen and her egg. In the lower part of the glen some rice stood that had not been garnered and he took the few grains to tempt the temple pigeons, thinking that perhaps they might catch one or two at a time and eat them. Then he returned to the temple with his plunder. Fortunately the priests in their flight had left their charcoal brazier and some fuel, also a few primitive dishes for cooking. The foreign doctor had a box of matches which he always kept in a waterproof case and was able to light a fire, so that night they did not fare so badly; but if their exile was to be of long duration there was a strong chance that they would starve.

Three days and nights they spent in such fashion and then it seemed necessary to get some information or make some move. The Great Helpful Lady had caught a severe chill as a consequence of the exposure, and now her symptoms made them fear pneumonia, and it was imperative to obtain some warm covering for her.

Many plans were discussed, but they finally agreed upon one suggested by Lao Pong. As soon as darkness fell he was to start for the neighboring market city, and buy supplies and food. A man who had been cured at the hospital lived in that place and he was an earnest inquirer into the new doctrine and very grateful as well, so they felt that he would assist them. It was a hazardous undertaking but the brave Lao Pong started out as if it were a pleasure excursion. In fact, he refused to allow the foreign doctor to attempt the trip, knowing that his master could never disguise himself from the curiosity of a crowd.

"It would be death to you, but to me it is mere child's play," lied the faithful fellow.

Yet several years later, the captain of an ocean steamer, on which the doctor traveled, spoke in the most contemptuous terms of the Chinese race.

"They are a dirty, dishonest, thieving set of beggars," the man announced. "There is not one of them I would trust around the block."

Lao Pang's cheery face and unselfish acts, and the noble death of Pastor Meng, flashed into the doctor's mind, and he afterwards confessed that never in his life had he been so tempted to knock a man down.

But to return to Lao Pong's adventure. It was a moonlight night when he set forth and he had the advantage of being able to see his path throughout the length of the valley. He was inwardly pleased at this, for the tales told of enchantment to the unwary traveler had made a deep impression on his mind, and he did not care to be made the victim of any spirit's jokes. He reached the town in the early morning when the farmers and merchants were bringing their produce into market, and among all the strangers he caused no comment. Without much difficulty he found the house of his friend, who treated him with every courtesy, notwithstanding the fact that he did so at the risk of his life. The man readily promised to make Lao Pong's purchases for him and bring back the news of the street. He was gone a long time and when he returned his report was not encouraging. The antiforeign feeling had spread throughout that region and search parties were out through the countryside looking for the refugees. An order had been pasted on the city gates to the effect that strangers were to be questioned and watch men placed at the entrance of all the mountain passes.

Lao Pong decided that the boldest course might in the end be the least suspicious. He had been forced to buy a donkey to carry his numerous purchases, and he decided to seat himself upon it in true Chinese fashion and join a caravan of merchants who were just starting for the City of the Blue Pagoda. He took good care to bring up the rear where he could leave the party at any moment should the necessity arise. In this manner he reached the entrance of the Spirit Valley. There the nature of the road forced the caravan to separate a little and he easily fell behind the rest for dusk was closing, and unnoticed he took the path turning to the temple.

He was received very warmly by his friends who eagerly inquired of his journey and the news he brought. It was not reassuring and when he reluctantly told them of the death of Pastor Meng, they were almost overcome. Their lives had been saved thus far, but at what a cost!

It was very apparent that they must remain where they were for some time to come; indeed the Great Helpful Lady's condition would allow of nothing else.

Her fever was raging, and at times she was delirious, going over and over her terrifying experiences.

The donkey, too, proved a cause of anxiety, for whenever a caravan appeared in the valley he would lift up his voice and salute his kindred. It was finally decided to hide him in the mouth of the cavern, where he would be out of sight and hearing from the road.

The following week Lao Pong made another attempt to reach the market town, but he was caught by some rough fellows at the top of the pass and escaped with the utmost difficulty. He was gone a day and a night, and the refugees had given him up for lost, but the following evening he returned weary to death from his wanderings in the mountains. Three weeks went by and four, and the Great Helpful Lady was slowly beginning to mend. Old Scarred Face, too, was evidently much better and from the intelligent look in her eyes they were sure that she knew what was passing, but she refused to speak. Her arm and rib had knit and the wounds on her head healed over and she seemed able to move the upper part of her body, but her symptoms showed that she was paralyzed below her waist, probably from the injury to the spine. They felt safe, therefore, where she was concerned. The beggar woman could not bear to have Hsie Yin near her and once, when the young woman brought her some food, she looked so threatening that from that time forward she left the care of her to the others.

Thus the days went on to the end of the fourth week. Every few days Lao Pong would make a fruitless attempt to get some news, but he always found suspicious characters crawling near and would be forced to return. Matters were growing desperate; the stores which he had gotten at the market city were just about exhausted and they were all carefully rationed. Lao Pong at length made the desperate resolution of going to the City of the Blue Pagoda and appealing to the young Lord Chang for aid. Bravely he started out and his friends remained behind, sad in the thought that his life might fall a sacrifice to his loyalty as Pastor Meng's had done.

Long before they expected him, he returned and with him were three chairs and their bearers. The fugitives could scarcely believe their eyes but Lao Pong's joyful shout reassured them. As soon as he could recover his breath, for he and the coolies had run almost all the way, he told them his joyful tidings.

"I have seen Wang Dah Mah and the young Lord Chang, and they have sent their greetings" he explained. "The Governor of the Province and the American Consul are in the city investigating the riots. Lord Chang has committed suicide and Creeping Sin is banished from the kingdom forever!"

# Chapter XIII
# Lord Chang Eats Bitterness

> O, silkily murmured Creeping Sin,
> "This is the stone you wished to win."
>    But in his ear the tall thin man
> Whispered with slow, strange lips—we knew
> Not what, but Creeping Sin went blue
>    With fear; again his eyes began
> To slant aside; then through the porch
> He passed, and lit a tall, brown torch.
>
>           —Alfred Noyes.

The hours that had dragged so wearily in the ruined temple had flown very swiftly in the City of the Blue Pagoda. The days were scarcely long enough to accomplish all the evil designs of Creeping Sin and Lord Chang. These two worthy companions had found one another's company so congenial that they had thrown all caution to the winds and were seen constantly together. Creeping Sin unceasingly fawned on Lord Chang and in this manner the wily intriguer wound his devious way into the confidence of the nobleman.

Evil times had fallen on the city. Looting and disorder had followed the riot, for Creeping Sin and Lord Chang secretly encouraged the rougher element in terrorizing the more respectable merchants and gentry, because they reaped a share in the profits.

At first Creeping Sin was convinced that the foreigners had perished miserably in the caverns and he imparted his conjectures to Lord Chang, withholding, however, all mention of Old Scarred Face. They felt it wiser, nevertheless, to keep up some form of pursuit, in case their enemies were somewhere in hiding, and when a beggar brought in word that Lao Pong had been seen at the market town in the vicinity, they renewed their efforts to catch the fugitives. The head official of the district, who was completely in Lord Chang's power, very willingly posted notices against the barbarians on every gate and blank wall, and had messengers sent through the neighboring towns offering rewards for the return or capture of the refugees.

The more decent people in the city soon grew tired of all these disturbances and wrote of the condition of affairs to the Viceroy of the Province. A friend of the foreigners also notified the American Consul, who lived on the great river, telling him of the disappearance of his fellow citizens and the fear that they had been murdered.

One evening, about a month after the first riot, a yamen runner, who was in the pay of Creeping Sin, came to his house and demanded entrance. He was received by his employer with the usual sneer reserved for inferiors.

"I did not summon you to-night; I told you to come to-morrow. You shall be bastinadoed for this presumption. Only fools come where they are not wanted," Creeping Sin threatened.

"As you will," whined the spy, "but you will lose information that you would pay a king's ransom to obtain."

"Speak out, then, and do not waste time that is worth more than gold," replied the Spider.

The fellow then hastened to explain that a secret message had just arrived for the chief official announcing that the Viceroy and the American Consul were on their way to investigate the riots and would reach the city the next day.

"You know it is not healthy for the body or the pocketbook to insult foreigners at present," said the man with an insinuating leer.

"When I want wisdom I will not seek it from a knave like you," snarled Creeping Sin. "Who says I am connected with this affair, I will throw their bones to be eaten by dogs."

"It is in everyone's mouth that you were seen at the mouth of the caverns talking to Old Scarred Face the night the foreigners disappeared. Since then you and Lord Chang are always together and the pigs on the street know what he thinks of the 'foreign devils.'"

For once Creeping Sin let his rage master him and he leaped at the man's throat.

"If you kill me, you will not hear the remainder of the story," gasped the man. Creeping Sin let his hand fall and stood glaring at he informer.

The man fold his tale in a straightforward manner that proved its truth. He had received his information from a servant of the Viceroy who had come to prepare the way for his master. The most carefully guarded secret is never safe in China; servants and underlings know a royal mandate to their masters some hours before those in authority receive it themselves. In this manner it had become known that the Empress Dowager was in a towering rage over the news of the antiforeign riot in the City of the Blue Pagoda. She was at that moment trying to establish more friendly relations with the great powers of Europe and America and this incident might endanger these negotiations and prove that she was acting in bad faith. She was particularly incensed with Lord Chang and had issued a command at the hand of the Viceroy that Lord Chang should appear at once at the capital, bringing with him Hsie Yin and the foreigners, as her majesty wished to decorate them for the fine work they had done during the cholera epidemic. If he did not obey immediately, his life and estate would be forfeited.

Creeping Sin could scarcely refrain a smile at the skill with which the wily Empress had laid her plans. Whatever happened Lord Chang would "lose face" and become the laughingstock of the Empire. To command him, of all people, to honor the barbarians was a clever bit of irony.

The man continued his story and Creeping Sin's smile soon disappeared. The Empress Dowager had watched Creeping Sin's evil practices for many years—in fact it was widely reported that he had paid the throne a large fortune to continue them—and now her patience was exhausted. She therefore banished him from the Flowery Kingdom for the duration of his life; a price of ten thousand taels was put on his head, and all his possessions were to be confiscated by the throne.

Creeping Sin was stupefied! Here was a plot cleverer than he had ever conducted against others. He did not, however, let the man see how deeply the report had moved him, but paid him liberally and sent him away.

Without delay Creeping Sin ordered a sedan chair called and set off to see Lord Chang, and on the way he thought over a scheme by which he could have his revenge on his old foe.

Lord Chang received his ally in the friendly fashion he had assumed toward him since their recent transactions. During the first hour of the visit Creeping Sin kept the conversation on pleasant topics. They sipped their tea and chatted over various events in the city and the plans which they had on foot. Creeping Sin very gradually brought the talk around to the Viceroy's intended visit. He told Lord Chang the reason for the official's coming and then went on to recount the news that the spy had brought, but made no mention concerning his own banishment.

"It is most unfortunate that the plot about the foreigners should have become known. I covered up the tracks so carefully that I cannot see who the betrayer could be unless it might be the careless word of a wayward boy. I am inconsolable that this disgrace should fall upon your honor, whose friendship is my most precious possession. I am the more inconsolable because I fear the

Empress Dowager's indignation will be even deeper when she knows that it is your own daughter whom you have treated in this manner."

"My own daughter? What right have you to mention my daughter? It is heaping indignity and insult upon me and my ancestors," cried Lord Chang, for once startled out of his accustomed calm.

"Nevertheless, this Dong Hsie Yin, the Chinese woman doctor, is your own daughter, Little Small-Feet, whom you refused to ransom. It will take a great amount of explanation to make Her Royal Highness understand that," sneered Creeping Sin. "Old Scarred Face and I have proofs enough and we have ways of bringing the matter to Her Majesty's ears that will keep us out of the trouble."

"A present between friends will often keep such matters quiet," answered Lord Chang. "I have many affairs to attend to this evening, and it will be quicker to name your price with no more conversation."

"Half of your possessions must be handed over to me before the sun rises, and a letter written to your agents in the Strait Settlements empowering me to draw on you at my pleasure," demanded Creeping Sin.

"You will ruin me," exclaimed Lord Chang, to whom the thought of paying out so much money was worse than all the other troubles combined.

"You are ruined already," consoled Creeping Sin. "It would take all your fortune, large as it is, to make the Empress receive you now."

The men talked and bargained until nearly midnight but could come to no agreement. Creeping Sin saw that the nobleman was desperate and finally compromised on a large sum to be paid by Lord Chang's bankers in the Straits Settlements. The plotter would never have made these terms but he had his own affairs to set in order and time was precious. With great formality and courtesy he made his parting bows; men like Creeping Sin may forget their morals, but in the presence of their superiors in rank they seldom forget their manners.

Overwhelmed by the bad tidings Creeping Sin had brought, Lord Chang sat thinking until nearly daybreak. He had no reason to doubt the truth of his foe's assertions; there were too many proofs brought out in the course of their conversation to do that. As soon as his guest had departed, a servant entered and told his master that the Viceroy was expected to arrive. Something in the fellow's manner made the nobleman suspect that he, too, had heard the rumor of coming disgrace.

Various schemes occurred to the desperate man's mind, but only to be cast aside as worth less. It was evident that his pride was to be humbled to the dust and he was to be held up to the ridicule of the Empire. If ever a man "ate vinegar"

Lord Chang did so throughout those midnight hours. According to the ideas of his class, only one course lay open to him whereby he could save his "face." If he should take his own life, the blame for his action would be thrown on his enemies and his honor would be shielded; his respect for his ancestors and the good of the family demanded this sacrifice.

Very calmly Lord Chang prepared for the deed. Stretching himself on his couch he extracted from his pocket a tiny phial containing some small pellets of opium. Without the tremor of an eyelid he swallowed the contents of the bottle, and then from a table beside him he took his opium pipe. With the fatalism of the Orient he drew in deep drafts of unconsciousness; it was not strange that in his death Lord Chang should turn to his only remaining friend. After this manner did Little Small-Feet's father seek the shades of his ancestors.

The mourning of the Chang family made up in pomp what it lacked in sincerity. The two hundred servants were dressed in white and their sober faces showed no trace of the inward relief that they felt over the removal of their oppressor. The hired mourners did their part with zeal and unction, and their loud wails and ear-splitting shrieks attested to the city that a very great nobleman had passed.

The first three days after his death Lord Chang's spirit was supposed to spend in calling at the various temples, in order to receive cards of merit or blame for the deeds done in this life to carry with him on his journey. On the third day his spirit returned to his home for a farewell visit, and it is much to be feared that in his case the bundle of demerits must have been a heavy burden for a shade to carry. At this time the most important ceremonies occurred, and invitations to the "third day exercises" were issued to all the prominent people in the city. The Viceroy, who had come to degrade the nobleman, attended to do honor to his greatness, and many lesser officials knocked their august heads on the floor before his bier. Only Creeping Sin was conspicuous by his absence.

Lord Chang's trip to the land of shadows must certainly have been easy, to judge from the number of paper houses, chairs, beds, and furniture of every description, that were burned at his grave. Plenty of paper money, sedan chairs, and even an imitation opium pipe went up into the flames. Nothing was spared to make, him comfortable and happy.

For forty-nine days prayers were said by every variety of priest, and all business and pleasure were laid aside while the whole household mourned. When this time had elapsed the relatives could gradually resume their former occupations, but once a week, at least, there must be wailing beside the grave, and for twenty-nine months his son was supposed to stay in retirement, that he might show sufficient respect to his father's memory.

The tragic end to Lord Chang's career made no impression on Creeping Sin. The night after their momentous interview was spent in preparation for a speedy departure, for there was no use in waiting to hear the sentence of banishment read. For years Creeping Sin had been preparing for such an event, and it did not take him long to make ready. He ordered the dwarf to burn the premises as soon as his master had departed, for the wily plotter was determined that the Empress Dowager should reap as little benefit as possible from the confiscation of his goods. Just as the sun rose, his task was completed and Creeping Sin entered his sedan chair and was carried to the city gates. His road lay past the Chang residence and at the moment when his chair came opposite the entrance, the first loud wail arose which announced the nobleman's death. A smile of triumph lit up the features of Creeping Sin; his enemy was punished at last; he had paid the price for all his arrogance.

No one knew very definitely what became of Creeping Sin. One thing was certain: he never returned to the City of the Blue Pagoda. Rumor said that he had settled somewhere in the Straits Settlements, although some maintained that he was reaping a fortune on the coast of Africa. When the Chinese Republic was established and the old order swept away, many thought that he might purchase a pardon and return to his own country, but he was too dangerous a man to be desired by any party and his banishment was not repealed.

After the Great War broke out and the famous Emden raided the waters of the Far East, it was reported that a Chinese merchant who closely resembled Creeping Sin had been arrested at Penang for sending searchlight messages to the German captain. A secret arrest and trial followed but the findings of the court were not announced, so it was not known by the outside world what sentence was passed on the prisoner.

One morning, as the sun came up in splendor over a tropical sea, a firing squad stealthily crept through the palm trees down to where the surf was beating along the shore. Swiftly and in a businesslike manner they accomplished their errand: a shot rang over the water, then all was quiet but the breaking of the waves. Perhaps these men could solve the mystery of Creeping Sin's fate, but military discipline keeps them discreetly silent.

# Chapter XIV
# "The Old Order Changeth"

> We have come by curious ways
> To the Light that holds the days;
> We have sought in haunts of fear
> For that all-enfolding sphere:
> And lo! it was not far, but near.
>
> We have found, O foolish-fond,
> The shore that has no shore beyond.
>
> Deep in every heart it lies
> With its untranscended skies;
> For what heaven should bend above
> Hearts that own the heaven of love?
>
> —Alfred Noyes.

The great gates of the city stood wide open on the day of Little Small-Feet's return. Wheelbarrows full of supplies and donkeys loaded with merchandise jostled each other in the entrance way. On a stool beside the road a man was having his head shaved, for in this region the barber shops were in the open air and the hairdresser and his patron had ample opportunity to watch the passing show and comment on the traffic, and many titbits of news they rolled around their tongue.

With beating hearts the fugitives approached the spot. What would be their welcome to this city from which they had been so rudely turned out? Thus far they had been able to avoid attention for there had been few passers-by, but now the observant street gamins would surely notice them. Were they to be insulted and jeered at or would the presence of the Viceroy keep the citizens respectful? Only time would tell.

The barber was the first to catch sight of the foreign doctor and he nearly dropped his razor in his surprise. He immediately forgot his waiting customer and running forward made a respectful bow to the stranger.

"Are you returning to our unworthy city?" he inquired deferentially. It was evident that the barber was exceedingly anxious that no suspicion of having joined the mob should cling to him.

Others then pressed forward, welcoming the party and even going so far as to invite them to stop and take tea. Women ran to their doors and stood there smiling and bowing, and when an unlucky urchin raised the cry of "foreign devils" his mother promptly boxed his ears and hustled him into the house. With the death of Lord Chang and the disappearance of Creeping Sin, the whole atmosphere of the city seemed changed and the people breathed more freely.

"I have always maintained," said Li Sao Tze, who was apt to repeat to herself, "that the foreigners were beneficial with their good deeds. If it had not been for them I should never have seen again. Lord Chang never tried to cure my eyes. The people do well to show the doctors every honor, but all this politeness will not bring back Pastor Meng."

The same thought often occurred to the friends as they sadly took up their work. At every turn they missed Pastor Meng's wise counsel and his bright, happy face. No one ever could take his place and for days they could scarcely mention his name because his loss lay so heavy on their hearts.

The hospital had been very thoroughly looted, but the Viceroy had issued an order that if the culprits wished to avoid punishment, all stolen goods must be returned. The result was that before the friends reached the hospital much had been brought back. Under the cover of darkness there would be a knock at the compound gate, and when it was opened the person who had knocked would have disappeared and a bedstead, a mattress, or a table would block the way. In this manner a great deal of the property was restored and Wang Dah Mah spent her time in bringing order out of chaos.

It would be impossible to do justice to the warmth of Wang Dah Mah's greeting as she stood at the gate with tears of joy running down her face.

"The angels have again guarded you, have they not, Dong Hsiao Dje?" she exclaimed. When Old Scarred Face was lifted from her chair and carried into the hospital, the amah's countenance was a study.

"Why did you not leave her to die? She is no good to anybody and the world would be a better place without her!" the old amah cried.

"We could not do that. You know who set us the example of forgiving our enemies," answered Little Small-Feet, as she directed the men how to handle the injured woman more gently.

The day was crowded with cares. Visitors and cards of congratulations poured in and there was scarcely time to eat. The Viceroy and city officials sent messengers to inquire after the health of the foreigners and also contributed large subscriptions to the hospitals and said that the following day they would come in person. There was no doubt about it: there was a new spirit abroad.

On the first evening a man came to the compound gate and asked to see the doctor on important business. He was given admission and conducted to the doctor's office; after the usual bows and mutual inquiries for each other's names and health, he told his errand.

"I have come to make a confession," he said simply, "and to tell of the last words of Pastor Meng. I do not know whether you will ever forgive me for being present, but even if you do not, I must speak and rid myself of a burden that is choking me," and he made a gesture at his throat as if he were actually strangling.

"I will not make excuses but plainly say that I was with the mob, for the excitement on the street seemed to carry me away. When I entered the compound and saw that the people were mad for slaughter, I turned to leave. At that moment the stone was hurled that struck Pastor Meng and he fell almost at my feet. I heard him say, 'Oh, I see Jesus, I see Jesus,' and I have never seen a human face shine as did his at that moment. Who is this Jesus whom he spoke about and what is the doctrine that will make a man lay down his life so gladly for his belief? A religion that will give a man such courage is the religion that I want. Will you not give me the secret of its power? When I have found out about it, I am willing to be punished, but first let me learn this great truth."

The doctor talked to the man until late into the night and his eager mind seemed fairly to drink in the message.

"May I ask," the stranger inquired as he rose to leave, "if all the Christians in your country are men of burning hearts like Pastor Meng?"[1]

"Men like Pastor Meng are rare in any country," the doctor said sadly.

Another and a frequent visitor was young Lord Chang, now Lord Chang in his own right. Whenever he could steal away from the lengthy mourning at home, he would come to the foreign doctor and consult him about many questions. His father had left a huge fortune, far larger than anyone had supposed, and a good third of the land in the city belonged to the estate. The young man had decided to keep enough to support the family according to their rank, and the remainder

---
[1] Dr. Speer reports that a question like this was actually asked a foreigner after the Boxer uprising.

he wished to use for the benefit of his country. He had made up his mind that to administer such a vast sum to the greatest advantage he must have a foreign education, and he consulted the doctor about what courses he should take and where he should study. Pastor Meng's death had also had a profound effect upon him.

"I have never been so impressed by anyone as I was by him. I knew as soon as I saw him that he had something I had not. Since his death I hear from many quarters the kindnesses he did in many quiet ways for the poor. I want to be trained so that I can be like him and teach others the way he did. My country lacks leaders of unselfish purpose, who will gladly lay down their lives for the sake of a great cause. China's greatest need to-day is men of burning hearts like Pastor Meng."

The doctor was much impressed by the fact that two such different types of people had described the impression Pastor Meng had made on them in exactly the same words. These expressions of praise were on all the people's lips in the next few days. The foreigners were surprised to discover how widely Pastor Meng was known and how many acts of kindness he had done in the short months he had been in the city. One of the women came with a gift of a few cash for the rebuilding of the chapel.

"I am very poor," she said, and indeed she looked it, "but I want to give what I can to help the work Pastor Meng loved. He sat up all night with my husband when he was so bad with the cholera, and he would take no pay. The poor of the city have lost a great friend."

Life at the hospital resumed its usual course, and now that the people had lost their prejudices, the wards were full. Young Lord Chang had offered to give the foreigners a fine piece of property in the highest part of the city, on which they could erect hospitals, schools, and residences, and the friends were soon deep in plans and contracts.

Lord Chang evinced his interest in all these plans by making many useful suggestions and by helping to engage the best workmen the city afforded. Wang Dah Mah was equally interested and came almost every day to help in the wards. One blustery winter day Wang Dah Mah left the palace and took the usual road to the hospital. On the preceding morning Hsie Yin had visited Lady Chang at the latter's request and had prescribed for her cough. Wang Dah Mah wished to hear of the result of the examination away from her mistress's presence so, glad of an excuse to see Hsie Yin, whom she admired more than anyone else in the world, she decided to go to the foreign compound and make her inquiries there.

"O Wang Dah Mah," Little Small-Feet exclaimed, as she greeted her favorite with out stretched hands, "I am sure that I can help your lady. Her cough is not serious; the trouble is with her spirits; she seems to be very, very sad. Did she love Lord Chang so dearly, that she should grieve like this?"

"That is not the trouble, Dong Hsiao Dje. No member of his family could really mourn for him; the house is a pleasanter place now that he is gone. Lady Chang has been sorrowful these many years because a little daughter was drowned in the river and she has never been interested in anything since that day. The priests in the temple told her that the child was not a real human being but a changeling and that she ought to be glad that she is gone. We know better now, you and I, and I have been telling my mistress about what you taught me and that is the reason she wanted to see you. You will go often, will you not, and tell her that sometime or other she will see the child again?" pleaded Wang Dah Mah.

"Indeed, I will, if your mistress wants me. I loved her from the moment I saw her; there is something that is very wistful and appealing about her. Is it not strange that the palace and the gardens seemed very familiar to me? I knew without being told where I should find the summer house and the view of the river and the pagoda seemed like a long-forgotten dream. I suppose they must be like some of the gardens in the City Lying in the Shadow of Purple Mountain, but I am sure that there was no pagoda there. I must ask my lady about it."

Wang Dah Mah could give no solution to this problem, and seeing that Hsie Yin was busy she turned her footsteps toward the wards, for there was nothing that the amah liked better than to go from bed to bed, talking to the patients and telling them the good news that had wrought such a change in her life. When she entered the room she hesitated to whom she should go first. Several women beckoned to her, and Old Scarred Face who lay near the door made no sign, but there was a fierce questioning look in her eyes that drew Wang Dah Mah irresistibly to her side.

The good soul had made up her mind, when she saw how Hsie Yin treated Old Scarred Face, that if she who had been so grievously wronged could act in such a forgiving spirit, she herself certainly could. So for several weeks she had gone to the beggar in exactly the same way she had to other women, and would bring her book and read little bits out of the Gospels. Old Scarred Face was anything but responsive, but she did not revile her for doing it, and Wang Dah Mah took that as a favorable sign and continued her efforts. Sometimes she went so far as to bring the sick woman a flower, an orange, or a sweetmeat, and she noticed that at last

Old Scarred Face seemed to watch the door and her face would brighten when she saw the old amah approach her. When she drew closer, the cloud would again fall, however, and she would greet her visitor with the old sullen look.

This evening for the first time, Old Scarred Face volunteered a remark.

"What makes them do it? What makes them do it?" she said huskily, as if forced by some inner compulsion to speak against her will.

"Do what?" asked Wang Dah Mah bewildered.

"Take me in and care for me when they must hate me the way I do them. They are certainly mad; or are they just trying to make me well so that they can torture me afterwards? I wish that they would kill me at once and be done with it," said the beggar woman.

Wang Dah Mah nearly laughed in her face; the thought of Dong Hsiao Dje killing anyone was too absurd.

"They are not going to murder you; they are trying to make you well. They are benevolent people and to hate anyone is not their custom. Their religion tells them to return good for evil. That is how the Great Teacher taught them to act," the amah answered.

"Who is this Teacher you are always talking about and where did he live?" questioned Old Scarred Face, thinking that here she might find solution to the mystery.

"He came to earth to teach us how to live, and he died for all the world," said Wang Dah Mah.

"But what made him die?" asked the beggar woman. "Tell me all about it."

"Ah, that is the story that hurts the heart!" exclaimed Wang Dah Mah sorrowfully. "Men would not receive the news of peace and rest he brought and he was done to bitter death by foes."

The short winter day was drawing to a close, and the long evening shadows were filling the room with odd distorted outlines; it was just the hour when one would talk intimately and softly of strange lands and unseen things; there in the twilight, in the picturesque language of the Orient, Wang Dah Mah told to this woman who was a sinner the story of the crucifixion. Old Scarred Face watched the narrator breathlessly and listened unconscious of anything else, while the amah with fast falling tears made the scene as vivid as if it had happened yesterday. It is hard for those who have always been familiar with it to realize the tragedy and beauty of the story as those do who hear it for the first time.

"You say this thing is true, and that our sins will be forgiven and that when we die we will go and live with that Great Teacher?" asked Old Scarred Face. "It is a strange tale and hard for an ignorant person to understand, but he was a good man, a good man!"

"Yes, it is true; but to be forgiven, we must repent of the evil things that we have done and try and do better," said Wang Dah Mah.

"That would be a miracle; I have been taught to hate everyone and look out for myself all my life; I am too old for anything else," and as if to prove her words, Old Scarred Face began to revile her acquaintances, particularly Creeping Sin.

"You should not talk in that dreadful manner," said Wang Dah Mah sternly. "Decent people will not stand it, how much less the great God in heaven!"

To Wang Dah Mah's surprise, Old Scarred Face took the rebuke quietly and made no reply. The two women had been so intent on their conversation that they had not noticed what was going on in the ward around them, but now Wang Dah Mah saw that it was time for the patient's supper so she rose to leave.

"It is a strange, strange tale," said Old Scarred Face once more. "I should never believe it for a moment if they had not treated me so well here. I should like to see that place you call heaven; I am very tired of wandering from place to place, and living in the hovels and caves is hard when one is old. Is it even better than the hospital?" she asked wistfully. "But I cannot change now."

"Yes, it is far, far better than the hospital, and it is never too late. Remember the man on the cross; he repented and received forgiveness. I must go now for here comes the nurse, but I will come to-morrow and tell you more."

In asking Old Scarred Face to repent and confess, Old Wang Dah Mah had unconsciously asked of the beggar woman the very hardest thing she could have done. A nurse at that moment spilled some broth on the bed and was startled at the string of dreadful oaths that were hurled at her. Wang Dah Mah looked at Old Scarred Face reproachfully but to no effect; a reaction had set in against her recent docility. Very much disappointed, Wang Dah Mah left the ward.

When Wang Dah Mah returned the following day, instead of receiving her with pleasure, Old Scarred Face scowled at her and refused to speak, and although the amah lingered for some time, she could get no word out of the beggar woman. Several days followed with the same result and it seemed as if Old Scarred Face had repented of having talked so freely and determined not to commit herself further. No one knew of the terrible struggle that was going on within her, a struggle between the evil she had always known and the tiny seed of good that had recently been planted. The doctors wondered why her heart should grow weaker and weaker and did not realize that it was the violent mental conflict that was shortening the woman's life. To give up hate for love, to substitute good will for malicious deeds, seemed impossible after so many years. Yet the fact remained, and Old Scarred Face admitted it to herself, that if she wished to enjoy any happiness in the future she must confess her misdeeds and try to repair the mischief she had done before she died. The scene on the cross had made a vivid impression on her mind and some words of Wang Dah Mah rang in her ears:

"If we do not repent and follow his teaching he will have died in vain so far as we are concerned."

The hours dragged on and the woman failed by the moment; it seemed impossible that she should live through another night, but her heart still beat on, and toward morning grew a little firmer. Finally, the nurse standing beside her bed thought she saw the sick woman's lips move. She bent over her to hear the words, for the voice that had been so coarse and harsh was very feeble now.

"Give me some of that medicine to make me strong and send for Wang Dah Mah; I have something to say to her," Old Scarred Face whispered.

The nurse did as she was asked and in the course of an hour Wang Dah Mah was beside the sick woman.

"Make all these people go away," commanded Old Scarred F,ace. "What I say to you, you may tell them yourself, but they shall not have the triumph of hearing me."

Wang Dah Mah told the nurse and the doctors what the woman had said and they at once with drew to the other end of the ward.

"I am too weak to tell the whole story; anyway why should I? The main facts are enough. This Dong Hsiao Dje, whom you think so much of, is Little Small-Feet. I stole her when I found her lost near the blue pagoda and held her for a ransom. Lord Chang—may the dogs tear his heart out in the place to which he has gone—refused to pay the money, so I kept her until the foreign lady adopted her." After this long sentence the woman paused for breath.

"Little Small-Feet? Little Small-Feet? Why, your mind must be wandering. Little Small-Feet was drowned in the typhoon; her father told us the story," exclaimed Wang Dah Mah, who could not believe her ears and thought that the woman must be inventing this wild tale.

"You may believe me or not, as you choose, but you know Lord Chang well enough to under stand that he would not love to pay a large ransom for anything, particularly for a daughter he did not desire. Here is a charm took from off the girl's neck when I sold her clothes. You probably made it yourself, so you ought to recognize it." Old Scarred Face then drew from out the garment she was wearing a charm such as young children carry to keep off the evil eye.

When Wang Dah Mah saw this, all her doubts were dispelled and she left Old Scarred Face to herself and hurried to where the others were standing.

"O Dong Hsiao Dje, Dong Hsiao Dje," she cried, "Old Scarred Face says that you are Little Small-Feet."

"Of course, I am Little Small-Feet, but only my lady calls me that now," replied Hsie Yin, surprised at Wang Dah Mah's excitement.

"Yes, but she says you are my Little Small-Feet, whom we all thought was drowned in the river, and your father was Lord Chang, but he would not pay a ransom, so Old Scarred Face kept you," answered the amah impulsively seizing Hsie Yin's hand.

They all returned to Old Scarred Face's bed, who told them in a feeble voice about her share in the kidnaping. As she talked, long-forgotten incidents flashed into Hsie Yin's mind which went far to confirm the story.

"Was it you, Wang Dah Mah," Hsie Yin asked, "who taught me the song about Little Small-Feet? It runs:

> 'The small-footed girl
>     With the sweet little smile,
>  She loves to eat sugar
>     And sweets all the while.
>  Her money's all gone
>     And because she can't buy,
>  She holds her small feet
>     While she sits down to cry.'"

"Yes, yes," laughed Wang Dah Mah; "I used to sing it to you sitting by the goldfish pool."

Old Scarred Face listened to them with an anxious scowl on her face, but her breath was growing labored and her hands cold.

"When are you going to put me into the street?" she faltered.

"Into the street? Why, what do you mean?" asked Hsie Yin.

"I thought, of course, you would throw me out when you had found what I had done. I would have turned you out like a dog if you had acted so to me. It is the custom here not to let people die in the house; it brings bad luck," faltered the beggar woman.

She had been so comfortable in the hospital; was it any wonder that her confession cost her a great effort when she feared such a result?

"We would not think of treating anyone in such a manner. We are too glad that you have told us to take such a mean revenge," said Little Small-Feet.

A great joy flashed over the dying woman's face; the hard lines were swept away and a gentler look came into the fierce glance.

"Oh, now I know you spoke the truth when you told the story of the Great Teacher, for you live his words all the time. I hated you because Lord Chang refused to pay a ransom for you, and I swore that I would have my revenge. We beggars are not taught goodness, as you know; we think that it makes people soft. Will you forgive me, for I never had a chance?"

Hsie Yin took the clawlike hand and raised it to her lips. At the touch of her lips Old Scarred Face smiled contentedly, then she closed her eyes and they thought that she would not speak again.

Suddenly, however, she returned to consciousness.

"I have just had a dream," she whispered, "and I saw hundreds of thousands of women and children clothed in rags and living in wretchedness, women and children exactly like you and I were, and they howled and swore and died out in the mountains and in their hovels. Is there no place like this for them? Will no one tell them about the Great Teacher?"

"We will do our best," sighed Little Small-Feet; "that is what we came here for."

"But you are so few and they are so many; their cries ring in my ears, because many of them I taught to lie and steal. Won't you tell more people in the great country beyond the seas about the beggars and their needs?" moaned Old Scarred Face.

Again she slept and they stood silent watching her; then, just as the first rosy fingers of dawn drew away the dark curtain of night, a bright smile lighted up her face; she drew one sigh of deep contentment and then, like the other penitent woman long ago, Old Scarred Face met her Master in the light of the early morning.

When all was over, Little Small-Feet turned to her old amah and said softly, "Now take me to my mother, Wang Dah Mah."

The Little Breezes Sway The Pagoda Bells With Gentle Fingers At The Sunset Hour

# Chapter XV
# A City Where Dreams Come True

> All the shores when day is done
> Fade into the setting sun,
> So this story tries to teach
> More than can be taught in speech.
>
> —Alfred Noyes.

Twelve years have passed since Little Small-Feet came into her own. Every March when gentle Spring and her little breezes travel northward, she finds new changes in the City of the Blue Pagoda and upon the mountain side. First, it was the huts that clustered around the old wall that had disappeared to be replaced by tiny houses and market gardens; the next season, she found that a large portion of the poorer section had vanished and very plain but sanitary buildings had taken the place of the hovels. Again, another year, street lights had been installed; and, finally, the hospitals and schools were completed; never before in the history of the Province had education been more popular. Business had improved, too, since opium-smoking and gambling had been abolished; the many junks, steam launches, and motor boats on the river told of the increased prosperity.

Hsie Yin and her brother, Lord Chang, have been given an opportunity that few reformers have had; the immense fortune their father left has made it possible to carry out the ideas that they received while studying abroad, and their gift for organization and reconstruction has kept them from the mistakes that idealists often make. They have wrought their changes gradually, so as not to arouse the hostility of a very conservative people, delaying improvements long after they were planned in order to carry public opinion with them. Their personal popularity, and the fact that it was members of their own race and not foreigners who were suggesting these ridiculous alterations, has helped very much to allay fears and break down prejudice.

"Oh, yes," the poor people say, with a shake of the head, "the great folks are wild for cleanliness and order; let them have it if they are willing to pay for it."

Of course the rougher element, the beggars and criminals, were much against these innovations and tried to make trouble, but young Lord Chang's prominent position made it possible for him to have them banished or punished and these disturbances ceased.

The foreign doctor and the Great Helpful Lady remained in the city for eight years; then the doctor broke down in health and was forced to return to his own country. Little Small-Feet has greatly missed their companionship. She has secured two foreign-trained Chinese doctors to fill their places, but the newcomers are at present too immature to be trusted with the full responsibility.

The work that is dearest to Hsie Yin's heart is that among the girls and beggar children. One of the prettiest and quaintest sights in all the world may be seen on the mornings when Little Small-Feet visits the kindergarten; the little tots cluster around her, clutching at her skirts and looking up into her face with adoring eyes, or draw their chairs in a circle to hear her tell them a story.

Has it paid to educate Hsie Yin? The women who sit by their doorways would give us their opinion if we could understand them. As of yore they have very decided opinions on a variety of subjects. But the legends which they tell their children in the dusk are quite different from those with which Wang Dah Mah used to frighten her darling; demons and evil spirits are slowly going out of fashion. Instead, they relate a tale about a brave man named Pastor Meng, who defied a mob and met a hero's death rather than betray his friends; but the story the children like best to hear is the story of a little baby born in a palace who was stolen by a wicked beggar and traveled all over the land until, finally, a kind lady found her and brought her up. Later, when she had become a beautiful woman, she dis covered her old home, becoming wealthy once more, but with all her riches she never forgot to be a friend to the poor. So every little boy decides to grow up like Pastor Meng and each tiny girl wishes to be a second Hsie Yin.

Little Small-Feet lives a very busy life, but whenever she does have an hour to spare, the place she likes best to visit is her father's garden. In the late afternoon Wang Dah Mah often finds her mistress in the summer house that overlooks the river. The sun touches the broad stream, showering its golden rays over the blue pagoda, then slips beyond the earth's rim, leaving a path of crimson in the sky.

"The bells are quiet to-night," Little Small-Feet murmurs.

"Yes;" Wang Dah Mah replies, "and they did not ring when you were born. That used to trouble me, but I know better now, although somehow even yet I feel more rested when I hear them ringing."

Perhaps the little breezes are listening to the old amah's words. It surely seems as if they must be, for they leave off romping down the garden paths and hurry to the river bank. There they sway the pagoda bells back and forth with gentle fingers and the music of the silver tones lulls the city to sleep.

"It must be the hands of angels," Little Small-Feet whispers. "No mortal touch could move the bells so softly."

We invite you to view the complete
selection of titles we publish at:

www.TEACHServices.com

Scan with your mobile
device to go directly
to our website.

Please write or email us your praises, reactions, or
thoughts about this or any other book we publish at:

P.O. Box 954
Ringgold, GA 30736

info@TEACHServices.com

TEACH Services, Inc., titles may be purchased in bulk for
educational, business, fund-raising, or sales promotional use.
For information, please e-mail:

BulkSales@TEACHServices.com

Finally, if you are interested in seeing
your own book in print, please contact us at

publishing@TEACHServices.com

We would be happy to review your manuscript for free.

www.ingramcontent.com/pod-product-compliance
Lightning Source LLC
Chambersburg PA
CBHW081922170426
43200CB00014B/2802